Weekend
WOODWORKING
with **POWER TOOLS**

Weekend
WOODWORKING
with POWER TOOLS

18 quick and easy projects • Stylish designs for your home

A L A N & G I L L B R I D G E W A T E R

NEW
HOLLAND

First published in 2006 by New Holland Publishers (UK) Ltd

London • Cape Town • Sydney • Auckland

Garfield House, 86–88 Edgware Road, London W2 2EA, United Kingdom

www.newhollandpublishers.com

80 McKenzie Street, Cape Town 8001, South Africa

14 Aquatic Drive, Frenchs Forest, NSW 2086, Australia

218 Lake Road, Northcote, Auckland

ISBN 1 84537 249 2

1 3 5 7 9 10 8 6 4 2

Editorial Direction: Rosemary Wilkinson
Senior Editor: Corinne Masciocchi
Production: Hazel Kirkman

Designed and created for New Holland by AG&G Books
Design: Glyn Bridgewater
Illustrations: Gill Bridgewater
Editor: Alison Copland
Photographs: AG&G Books

Reproduction by Modern Age Repro, Hong Kong

Printed and bound in Malaysia by Times Offset (M) Sdn. Bhd.

CONTENTS

INTRODUCTION

Sometimes when I am alone in the workshop – all nicely ensconced with lots of wood and tools all around – I think about how the craft has changed over the years. Not so long ago I was totally convinced that hand tools were the only way forward. I think that my initial reluctance to use power tools goes back to the early days when they were a bit of a horror.

I clearly remember my first one-does-all power tool. One moment I was excited about the notion of using an innocent-looking attachment that claimed to be able to cut dovetail joints, and the next moment it was unleashed and busy chewing, biting, clawing, scratching and mangling its way through my precious wood. After a day or so of buying yet more wood, wondering how best to protect my body parts, and generally trying to figure out where I was going wrong, I gave up.

The good news is that power tools have evolved to the point where they really do a marvellous job. So, where I was once excited about the exquisite way that steel, brass and wooden hand planes did their thing, I am now just as excited about power tools. Better still, the design standards have rocketed, and the prices have tumbled, to the point where average hobby woodworkers can easily kit themselves out with a whole range of top-quality tools. I am not advocating that you spend out on expensive items, but rather that you go for good-quality, low-cost tools – the sort of power tools that you see in every do-it-yourself (DIY) centre.

The intention of this book is to share with you the pleasures of using power tools to build projects from wood. At the beginning of the book, there is a comprehensive tools and techniques section that gives you all the information you need. Each project opens with a short introduction that tells you something about its inspirational origins, and then we go straight into the construction stages.

By the time you have made one or two items, there will be no stopping you. For example, once you have made the kitchen stool, there will be no reason why you cannot make a whole kitchen complete with worktops, cupboards and all the rest. So let the fun begin!

Before using power tools, read the manufacturer's instructions.
Always follow the manufacturer's guidelines on safe operation.

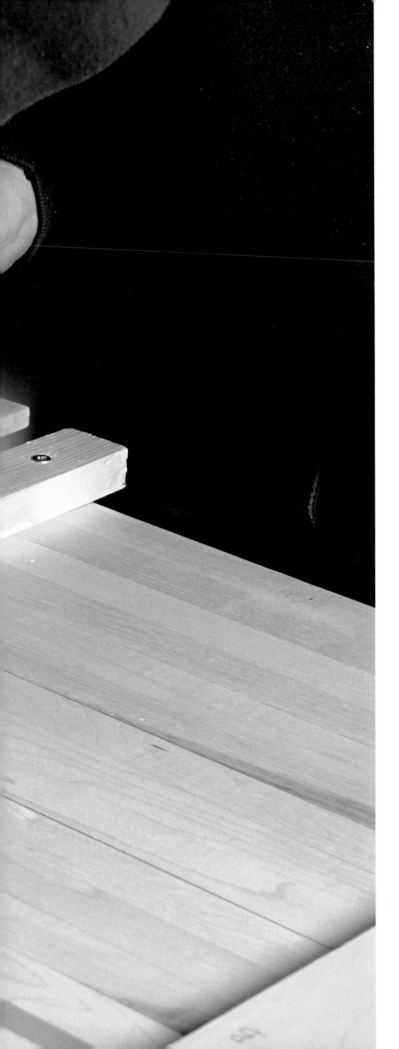

TOOLS, TECHNIQUES AND MATERIALS

Woodworking with power tools is an amazingly satisfying and fun activity, but only if you are confidently using the right tools, techniques and materials for the task. It is no good wrestling with the wrong type of jigsaw, or trying to use low-cost pine when you really ought to be using oak, and then thinking at the end of a long, bone-weary day that woodworking is not for you. If you choose your tools and materials with care, and if you take your time to understand the techniques, you will enjoy the experience. The best advice, when buying the power tools, is to start with a few must-haves like a good-quality cordless drill, a jigsaw, a sander and a mitre saw, and then get other items when the need arises.

WORKING EQUIPMENT

Power-tool woodworking – working with drills, drivers, orbital sanders, jigsaws, biscuit jointers and routers – is a wonderfully joyous, exciting and productive activity, but only if the work area is clean, well organized and, most importantly, safe. The following pointers will help you create a pleasant, user-friendly woodworking environment.

SPACE

If you do not have a workshop consider working outdoors or in a garage, shed or spare room. Materials need to be stored indoors to prevent them deteriorating.

FLOOR SURFACES

The floor must be dry, clean, hard-wearing and, above all, non-slip. Steps, changing levels, crumbling concrete and slick, shiny surfaces are hazardous.

AIR AND WINDOWS

Clean, fresh air and plenty of natural light are essential. When you are painting and varnishing, you must be able either to switch on an extractor fan or to open a window. And on a hot summer's day, it will be good if you can throw open a door or window or work outside.

WORKBENCH

To make sure that you work at the correct height, a workbench with a vice is ideal, but alternatively you can use one or two portable folding workbenches.

ELECTRICAL SAFETY

Power tools should not be used if the power tool cord is damaged or the connection to the plug is damaged. For added protection you can use a circuit-breaker (plug into the power socket and plug the power tool into the circuit-breaker). Modern electrical installations incorporate circuit-breakers and offer a safer working environment.

TOXIC MATERIALS

Many workshop materials, such as wood dust, and chemicals in paints and varnishes, are potentially toxic. Always follow the manufacturer's guidelines and always be aware of the potential problem of toxicity.

KNOWING YOUR POWER TOOLS

Always read the manuals and follow the guidelines. The following rules must be observed:
- Secure the workpiece prior to using a tool
- Keep your hands behind the cutting edge
- Work at an easy pace – no forcing or twisting
- Select the correct tool for the task
- No rushing – go at it slowly

DRESS FOR THE JOB

Tie up long hair, remove dangling jewellery and do not wear baggy tops or flapping sleeves.

DEBRIS

Things like wood dust, offcuts of wood, plastic bags, oily rags and dropped tools are all potentially dangerous. Clean up at the end of the day; sweep the floor and work surfaces and clean all the tools you have used.

TELEPHONE

The telephone is a good/bad item: good if there is an emergency, but bad if it rings when you are working. Just make sure, when it rings, that you switch off the tools and leave everything in safe order.

CHILDREN

Kids love watching woodworking. If you want your children to share in the fun, make sure they are safely kitted out, and that they can watch without being in harm's way.

EMERGENCIES

Never work when you are tired or under medication. Tell family and friends where you are. Never put your hands or eyes at risk. Make sure that there is an emergency number close to the telephone.

SAFETY EQUIPMENT

Goggles

Dust mask

Ear-defenders

GOGGLES

Woodworking is potentially dangerous – there will be splinters, wood dust and fragments of wood flying through the air. You must wear protective goggles, or better still, a full face mask. Get the best pair of goggles or face mask that is available, and use it!

DUST MASK

The fine wood dust created by power tools is dangerous; if inhaled, it is bad for the nose, mouth and lungs. At the very least, you must wear a particle-blocking dust mask. A respirator mask, with its own self-contained air-sucking filter, is a better option. Such helmet-type respirators are expensive, but they offer ear, eye and lung protection in a single unit.

EAR-DEFENDERS

Some woodworking tools are dangerously noisy, to the extent that long exposure to them results in ringing ears and general disorientation. All this can be avoided simply by wearing a pair of low-cost ear-defenders.

MEDIUM-DENSITY FIBREBOARD (MDF)

You could use MDF instead of plywood, but be aware that its use is possibly dangerous. Some experts consider that very fine MDF dust is potentially hazardous, much more so than dust from, say, hardboard or plywood. We prefer to use plywood even though it is slightly more expensive than MDF.

WOOD TYPES

Some woods are toxic. For example, some people have an allergic reaction when they handle iroko. We have chosen to use tried and trusted traditional woods such as maple and pine. The dangers associated with toxic wood are increased if the wood is ingested in the form of fine dust and comes into contact with moist membranes in the throat, nose and eyes. This is all the more reason why you should wear protection, keep the workshop clean, and follow health and safety guidelines.

SAFETY SUMMARY

Woodworking is potentially very dangerous. Always follow a safety checklist.

- Read the directions on products
- Read the machine manuals
- Spend time getting to know the tools
- Keep power tools in peak condition
- Keep your hair and clothes tied back
- Watch over children when they are in the workshop
- Keep the workshop locked when not in use
- Tell your family or a friend where you are
- Keep electrics in good condition
- Clean up dust and debris

KNOWING YOUR MATERIALS

A good part of designing with wood involves working within the limits of the material. If we take it that there are three primary factors – wood colour, wood texture, and the fact that wood expands and contracts in width and depth (the length stays the same) – then, to a great extent, design hinges on understanding the material options so that you can bring these three factors together for the best overall effect.

Ready-prepared pine is a good option, especially if you have no large machinery for cutting and planing rough-sawn wood.

READY-PREPARED WOOD

For the projects in this book, it is a good idea to get ready-prepared wood, meaning wood that has been planed and squared on all faces to a set width. You can even go one step further and order the wood sawn to a set length. Make sure, when you are ordering the wood, that you specify 'well seasoned' (see page 18), and that you go to a supplier who is able to machine the wood to a good finish. When it comes to using tongue-and-groove boards (as in the dog kennel on page 126), it is best to use top-quality prepared double-sided tongue-and-groove pine boards.

PLYWOOD

When making good-quality pieces with power tools, you should use multi-veneer birch plywood. This is expensive, but it is a beautiful material to work – it saws and planes to a clean, crisp edge, it is free from delaminations and knots, and the surface is attractive enough to leave in its natural state. Don't be tempted to use the soft-centre-type plywood boards. They will be a fraction of the cost of multi-veneer birch plywood, but they are almost impossible to cut to anything better than a fuzzy finish, they are dark in colour, and they cannot easily be finished with an edging strip.

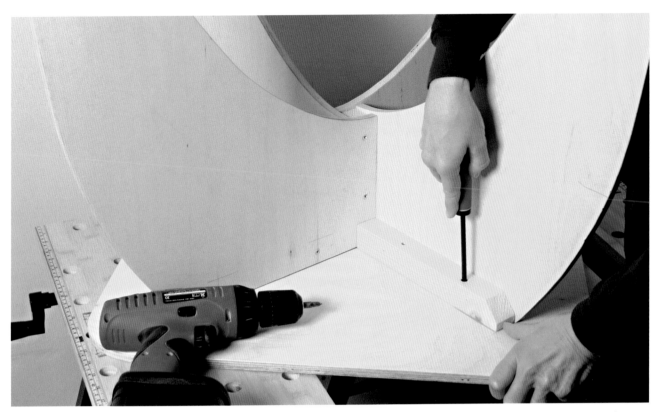

A manufactured board like birch-faced plywood can be used differently to solid wood; it is ideal for wide areas (as opposed to joining narrow planks of solid wood to make a wide board) and it expands and contracts far less than solid wood.

PINE

A coarse-grained, creamy-coloured softwood that is low in cost and easy to work, with an attractive texture and characterful knots – perfect for many of the projects in this book. Be wary of types that have large, loose, resinous knots that may fall out and ruin your project.

BLOCKBOARD

This product is made using many narrow sections (sometimes square-section 'staves') of pine, beech or birch, which are glued together to make a wide board. It is a good product for building the sides of chests and shelving. Blockboard is not as uniformly strong or stable as plywood but it does have all the benefits of solid wood – the edges are attractive, it can be re-planed and re-sanded if it gets scratched or dented, and it will gain character and last for many generations.

AMERICAN WHITE OAK

This commonly available hardwood is golden-brown in colour with a beautiful straight grain. It is very hard and consequently more difficult to work with than pine.

MAPLE

A creamy-coloured, even-textured, high-quality hardwood that is perfect for simple modern furniture.

AMERICAN CHERRY

A mellow, pink to brown, fine-textured, straight-grained hardwood that is suitable for finely crafted furniture.

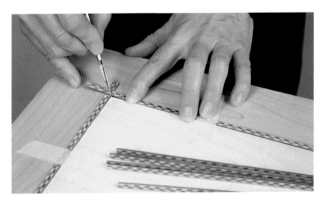

Consider combining materials. This coffee table uses 'white' birch-faced plywood, pale maple and a decorative band of contrasting woods.

STRUCTURE AND CONSTRUCTION

Much has been said over the years about how form ought to follow function but, when you really get down to it, both form and function ought to follow structure. To put it another way, start by sorting out just how the item needs to work and be put together, and then worry about how it needs to look.

EXPANSION AND CONTRACTION

When solid wood dries it shrinks (contracts), and when it becomes damp it expands – it is always changing in dimension. Although there is some change to the length of a board (meaning along the direction of the grain), it is so small that it can be ignored completely. Most of the 'movement' takes place across its width and its thickness (across the direction of the grain). These changes in dimensions are most noticeable in very wide boards or multiple boards glued together side by side; the width can change dramatically.

Over the years, techniques of construction have been developed to compensate for 'movement' in solid wood. For instance, if a door is made using a rectangular frame of narrow sections with grooves to hold a central loosely fitted panel, the height and width of the door will remain the same regardless of atmospheric conditions. Another example is the flexible joint needed for fixing a table top to the structure beneath (slotted brackets/plates are often used).

With pieces of woodwork that are going to stand out of doors in all weathers, such as a dog kennel or a piece of garden furniture, movement will be more noticeable. Consider using narrow sections and tongue-and-groove boards.

STRUCTURAL NEEDS

With most wooden structures – tables, chairs, cupboards – being essentially box-like in form, it is important that the 'box' is able to hold its shape without rocking, twisting, or catastrophically breaking down. Over the centuries, woodworkers have come up with ways of combating all the stresses and strains that we put on furniture. We use corner blocks to hold frames rigid and square, backs on cupboards to stop the top, bottom and side boards twisting and collapsing in on themselves, sticks and stretchers underneath chairs to help prevent the legs from twisting and/or spreading, diagonal triangulating braces to hold pieces square, complex joints to create right angles, and so on.

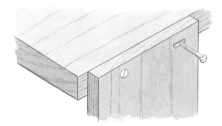

Screw and slot joints allow for dimensional movement across the grain.

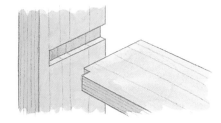

The stopped housing ensures that movement within the joint is hidden.

Traditional loose-wedged tenon construction allows the joint to be tightened when the wood shrinks.

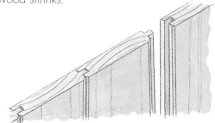

Tongue-and-groove construction disguises the inevitable movement.

Stools, chairs and tables need to withstand everyday use and abuse. Stools and chairs support 'dynamic' loads; the structure and joints need to resist rocking and twisting.

STABILITY

Although a chair or table has to be designed for ordinary everyday use – a chair must hold your weight, and a table must stand firm and be at the right height – they also, to some extent, have to be over-designed so that they can withstand misuse. For example, while we all know that chairs are designed for sitting on, we also know that people frequently sit on them incorrectly and will use them for standing on, and you need to take this into account.

Along with this over-designing for strength, you also have to design for safety. For instance, while a small side table is best designed so that it is low in height and wide across the base so that it will not fall over, the surface must not be so low, and/or the legs so splayed, that one or both become a hazard. Lastly, of course, a piece must not be so braced and strengthened that it is too heavy to lift, or just too ugly to live with.

LEVERAGE

When wide cupboard doors are opened to their full width, or the flaps on a table are opened up, there is a danger that your weight pushing on the door, or down on the table, will result in a levering effect, which in turn tips the piece over, or forces one part of the structure to lever and break another.

Either way, the levering effect can result in serious damage to the person doing the levering and/or the piece being levered. You must design the piece in such a way that the levering action cannot happen. You might need to fit stops on the doors, or have small doors rather than big ones, or design doors that slide rather than hinge.

Outdoor structures receive a battering from the elements. Reinforce the structure using triangulation and, where appropriate, set posts in the ground using concrete.

CONSTRUCTION PROCEDURES

Woodworking is like an exciting journey … you dream about the possibilities, you make plans, and then you systematically work through a series of procedures. Just like a wonderful journey, a large part of the pleasure of woodwork is in all the adventures that occur between start and finish.

CUTTING COMPONENTS TO SIZE

You can buy rough-sawn planks in various thicknesses from a timber merchant, select from a standard range of ready-prepared (planed) sections from a DIY outlet, or you can order finished components of any size from a specialist supplier. Rough-sawn boards need to be cut and planed to size; you will need a circular saw or band saw, a surface planer (jointer) and a thicknesser, so unless you have a large workshop we recommend that you buy prepared wood and cut to length as necessary. Manufactured boards can be purchased in various standard sizes (see page 142) but we recommend that you avoid buying 2440 x 1220 mm (96 x 48 in) sheets, which are difficult to handle.

CUTTING COMPONENTS TO SHAPE

To shape components, use the jigsaw for cutting broad curves in thick wood, and the coping saw for cutting fine curves in thin wood. To use the power jigsaw, clamp the workpiece to the bench, set the base plate on the wood, switch on the power and advance the tool to make the cut to the waste side of the pencil outline. To cut out a 'window', drill a hole through the waste, pass the blade through the hole, and make the cut as described. To use the coping saw, fit a new blade and adjust the tension. Clamp the workpiece to the bench, set the blade on the mark, and work the saw with a rapid up-and-down action.

JOINTING THE COMPONENTS

The component parts will need to be jointed (meaning cut with traditional joints like a mortise and tenon, rebates, grooves and the like, and/or fitted with screws, nails or other fixings – see page 34) so that they fit one to another. If you are working with expensive wood, cutting an unfamiliar joint or working with new tools, it is best to have a practice run on

A jigsaw is ideal for cutting out curved and complex shapes. It can also produce angled cuts (see page 21).

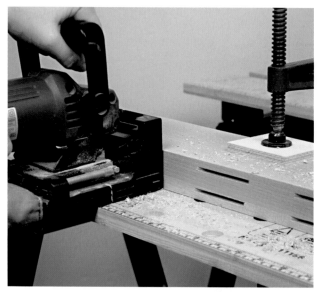

Biscuit joints are quick to make and are an effective way of joining boards edge to edge or at 90° (see page 33). Other angles can be achieved, depending on the biscuit jointer.

some scrap wood. It is also a good idea to sort out potential problems such as difficult joints, odd fixings or unusual constructions by making a swift prototype.

TRIAL DRY-RUN ASSEMBLY

Once you have got all the parts that go to make up the design, then comes the exciting stage of carrying out a trial assembly. The idea is to make sure that everything comes together properly, and to sort out any problems, before the gluing stage. Typically, you might have to ease a joint, tidy up a detail, repair a split or, if you have made a mistake, make a new part. Use easy-to-remove items like clamps, screws and patent fixings to hold the parts together.

SANDING

The sanding procedure involves using different grades of sandpaper to produce a smooth finish. You can hold the paper in your hand, either as a block or as a folded sheet, or you can use an electric sander. Start sanding only after you are satisfied that all the components are cut and shaped correctly and are ready to assemble. Use 80-grit sandpaper to clean and smooth the surfaces and to round over sharp edges and corners. Use an orbital power sander for large, flat surfaces. If you can only afford one type of power sander, it is best to choose a flat-bed-type orbital sander.

GLUING UP

Move to a dust-free area where the workpiece can be left for 24 hours. Carry out the trial dry run, making sure the parts fit together correctly. Set out the clamps, glue, bits of card and scrap, and work out the gluing order. Spread a small amount of white PVA glue on mating surfaces (both surfaces), clamp the parts up and leave overnight. Larger items, like the bar stool on page 64, might need to be glued up in two stages. Use a damp cloth to wipe away excess glue.

FINISHING

Finishing involves the process of sanding, sealing, colouring and polishing the wood surface, and bringing the work to a satisfactory conclusion. For a natural-looking finish that shows off the wood grain, we recommend using either Danish oil, teak oil, tung oil, or 'finishing oil'. After initial sanding with 80-grit sandpaper lay on a thin coat of oil (to seal the wood) using a white cotton cloth. Wait 24 hours, sand again using 600-grit sandpaper (or finer) and apply another thin coat of oil. To further enhance the surface you can apply wax polish after the second coat of oil has dried. For projects that come into contact with food, like the chopping board on page 52, either leave it plain or wipe it over with olive oil. If you are going to paint an item, use spirit-based oil paint or water-based acrylic paint (see page 39).

Cam dowel fixings (see page 34) are ideal for jointing cabinet-type structures and allow the item to be taken apart and reassembled as many times as you like.

When you have finished cutting and jointing, use an orbital sander and 80-grit sandpaper to smooth the surfaces and edges and to remove scratches, scuffs and pencil marks.

BUYING AND PREPARING WOOD

We get our rough-sawn boards from a timber merchant, and kiln-dried, sawn and planed softwood from a general DIY outlet. When we want top-class softwood or hardwood that has been machined to size, or anything slightly out of the ordinary, we go to a specialist wood supplier.

SAWN WOOD

If you want to cut costs and you don't mind all the time, sweat and effort involved in planing the wood to a good finish, you cannot do better than get sawn wood direct from a sawmill. Ask for 'well-seasoned' wood, meaning wood that has been sawn and air-dried. A board 25 mm ($^{31}/_{32}$ in) thick takes about a year to dry or season. Check the wood for problems, and avoid anything that looks twisted, split, stained, overly knotty or warped. You will need to get the wood oversize (about 6 mm ($^1/_4$ in) thicker) and then plane it back to a suitable thickness.

READY-PREPARED WOOD

Ready-prepared wood is well-seasoned wood (either air-dried or kiln-dried) that has been planed to size on all four sides. Most local DIY centres stock softwood in sections ranging from 32 x 12 mm ($1^1/_4$ x $^{15}/_{32}$ in) right up to 69 x 69 mm ($2^3/_4$ x $2^3/_4$ in) – perfectly suitable for about half the projects in this book. You will still have to cut it to length and occasionally adjust the size to suit your needs. If you want to give the planing a complete miss, go to a top-class specialist supplier and get them to machine the wood to a precise size (width, thickness and length) so that you only have to cut the joints.

Solid hardwood is the most beautiful and long-lasting of all wood materials and is worth the investment. Rough-sawn planks are cut and planed into smaller, smooth, straight and square components as required. Wide boards can be achieved by jointing narrow boards edge to edge.

Ready-prepared wood is available in a variety of sizes (see page 142). It has been planed smooth and is ready to cut to length. Consider also using decorative mouldings and dowels in your designs.

PREPARING WOOD

To prepare rough-sawn wood yourself you will need a workshop equipped with a circular saw (or a band saw), a surface planer (jointer) and a thicknesser. These are large machines that you should only consider buying if you intend taking up woodworking as a serious hobby or as a way of earning a living. Begin by cutting the plank into smaller pieces if appropriate. Create the first flat face using the surface planer. Plane the plank down to the finished thickness using the thicknesser. Plane the first flat edge using the surface planer and the 90° fence. If less than 150 mm (6 in) wide, plane the last edge using the thicknesser and if wider, saw the component parallel using the circular saw and plane using the surface planer.

BLOCKBOARD

Described variously as 'timberboard', 'stickboard', 'laminated board' and other names besides, blockboard is a board that has been built up from glued sections of wood. This is a really good material for items such as the top of the bar stool, the teddy bear chair and the hope chest – any project where you want a wide, stable board that has the same structural qualities as solid wood.

PLYWOOD

The projects in this book use top-quality birch plywood, sometimes called multi-ply. It is a sheet material made up from veneer layers and is easy to work – it saws and planes to a clean edge, the grain is light-coloured, and it oils and paints to an attractive finish. Once in place, it is strong and stable. Be aware, when you are looking at costs, that plywood comes in a whole range of grades and types – some top grade and faced with hardwood veneers, and others poor grade and full of knots, holes and splits.

OTHER SHEET MATERIALS

There are now lots of sheet materials on the market: everything from hardboard, chipboard and particle board through to soft-heart plywood and MDF (medium-density fibreboard). In the context of this book, where we are using low-cost power tools in a DIY home environment, we have opted to stay with a few tried and trusted types. The best advice, if you want to use another type of board, is to read up on its qualities, take note of any hazards associated with its use (such as dust or toxicity) and then have a go and see how it works out for you.

Manufactured boards such as plywood, MDF and chipboard are available in a variety of sizes and qualities (see page 142 for thicknesses).

COMPOUND MITRE SAWS

You can make straight and angled cuts with a hand saw or a jigsaw, but a compound mitre saw makes more accurate cuts. There are two options: a low-cost, fixed-head design (illustrated here), which is really good for cutting small sections, and a more expensive sliding-head design, which is good for most widths.

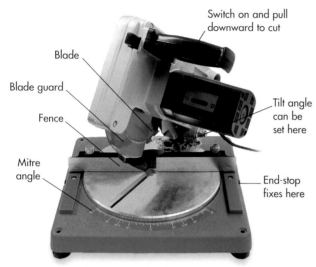

Switch on and pull downward to cut

Blade

Blade guard

Fence

Mitre angle

Tilt angle can be set here

End-stop fixes here

Compound mitre saw

During operation, always push the wood firmly against the fence and keep your hands as far away from the blade as possible. Never remove the blade guard.

CUTTING TO LENGTH

To cut a number of pieces to the same length, clamp the tool to the bench, fix the saw's end-stop to the required length (or clamp a wooden stop to some point on the bench), set the mitre and/or tilt angles to suit your needs, slide the workpiece hard up against the fence and along to the stop, switch on the power and make the cut.

CUTTING A BASIC 45° MITRE

To cut a 45° mitre, set the mitre angle either left or right to the 45° mark, and a perform a trial cut. Take extra care when making mitre cuts and keep your hands well away from the blade. When all is correct, draw a guideline on the workpiece to be cut. Set the workpiece on the saw table and against the fence, so that the line of cut is to the waste side of the drawn line, switch on the power and make the cut.

CUTTING A COMPOUND MITRE

To cut a compound mitre, set the saw blade to the required tilt and mitre angles, and perform a trial cut. Follow the same procedure as for a basic mitre. Take extra care while making compound cuts; you can use a stick to hold the wood in position rather than allow your hands near to the blade.

HINTS AND TIPS

- Always follow the manufacturer's instructions.
- Always wear goggles and a mask.
- When you are making adjustments to the saw, make sure that the power is switched off.
- If you have children, pull out the plug when the mitre saw is not in use, and lock the blade in the 'down' position.
- Always make a trial cut to verify that the tilt and blade angles are correct.
- Always make sure that you cut to the waste side of the drawn line.
- Always hold the workpiece hard down on the table and hard against the fence.

JIGSAWS

A jigsaw, sometimes called a sabre saw, is a good tool for the freehand cutting of straight lines and curves in any kind of wood. In use, set the base plate on the workpiece so that the blade is just short of the mark, switch on the power and advance the tool to make the cut.

CUTTING CURVES IN SHEET MATERIAL

To cut a curve in sheet material, hold the wood to be cut flat on the bench so that the line of cut is hanging clear of the bench, set the blade just clear of the mark, switch on the power and advance the saw at an easy pace. Make sure, all along the way, that the saw blade and the consequent line of cut is to the waste side of the drawn line.

More expensive jigsaws with a 'pendulum' setting are good for sawing thick materials.

MAKING ANGLED CUTS

The base plate can be tilted at an angle to the blade in order to produce angled cuts. This is sometimes done with an allen key underneath the saw. Extra care is needed when making angled cuts, since the blade will exit the wood in a different position than will be apparent. Make the cut in the same way as described above.

CUTTING A 'WINDOW'

To cut a 'window' or a hole, secure the workpiece in the vice or clamp it to a bench. Drill a pilot hole of 10 mm ($1\frac{3}{32}$ in) or more in diameter through the area of waste, and pass the saw blade through the pilot hole. Plan out how you are going to move the workpiece and/or the saw so that the blade is presented with

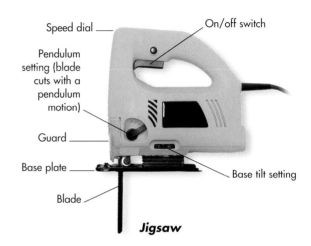

Speed dial — On/off switch
Pendulum setting (blade cuts with a pendulum motion)
Guard
Base plate
Blade
Base tilt setting

Jigsaw

the line of next cut – decide in which direction you are going to cut. Switch on the power and move and manoeuvre both the wood and the saw, all the while making sure that you are cutting slightly to the waste side of the drawn line.

When cutting curves, it is better to carefully rotate the saw to face the direction of the curve rather than attempting to force the saw in a sideways motion.

HINTS AND TIPS

- Always follow the manufacturer's instructions.
- Always wear goggles and a dust mask.
- When you are making adjustments to the saw, make sure that the power is switched off.
- Slow down the advance of cut when you are working around tight curves.
- Always hold the base plate part of the saw hard down on the workpiece.

- Always switch the power off and wait for the blade to stop moving before you remove the saw from the workpiece.
- Make sure that your fingers are clear of the line of cut.
- Keep your hands well away from the blade and be aware that a long blade and a tilted blade (for making angled cuts) pose a greater threat.

MEASURING AND MARKING

The success of a project – the way the component parts fit together – hinges on good measuring and setting out. If the faces and edges are square and true, the measurements are accurate, and you double-check along the way, the chances are that good sawing, planing and jointing will follow.

RULERS

There are all sorts of rulers: one-piece bench rulers, steel rulers, plastic rulers, and so on. I like using a traditional four-fold wooden ruler: it opens out to 1 m, and there are metric graduations on one edge and imperial ones on the other. A 1 m metal ruler is a good alternative and provides a straight edge for marking out. Metal rulers are also available in lengths of 600 mm (24 in), 300 mm (12 in) and 150 mm (6 in). These are all useful as it is much easier to mark out joints on small components using a small ruler.

TAPE MEASURE

The metal tape measure, or flexible measure, is a ruler consisting of a strip of spring steel that is wound into a small, handy container. In use, you pull the tape out, take the measurement and then release the tape, which automatically rewinds back into its case. The tape is good for measuring lengths longer than 1 m and for measuring curved profiles. The disadvantage is that the tape may become kinked and result in inaccurate readings. It is best to get a small tape – one that feels comfortable in your hand.

It is essential to mark out wood accurately. Use a ruler and a sharp pencil to do this. Before you start, check that your piece of wood is square (has 90° corners).

TRY SQUARE

The woodworker is continually needing to test or mark lines to ensure that faces or edges are at right angles (90°) to one another. There are many squares on the market – a combination square, a carpenter's square and one or two others – but the most useful square is known as a try square. The wooden stock (handle) and metal blade are at true right angles (90°) to each other. In use, the stock is held hard up against a true face (some part of the project being made) and lines are drawn against the blade.

AWL

This is a pointed tool used to spike holes and scribe a line for an accurate saw cut (across the grain). It is useful for marking a location point for the centre of a hole before drilling. It has a thin, needle-like spike and a ball-shaped handle. In use, the handle is cupped in the palm of the hand with the index finger pointing along the spike. The tool is either drawn to make a scratched line or swivelled to make a hole. A variation on the awl is a chisel-pointed version called a bradawl, which is used for spiking holes in hardwood.

MARKING OUT A RADIUS

For marking out a small radius, use compasses and a sharp pencil. For marking out a larger radius, use a trammel or 'beam compass'. You could get away with using large compasses with an extension bar, but a trammel does the job best. In use, set the points a distance apart – the distance being the radius of the circle or part-circle that you want to draw – then simply spike one point on the centre and move the other so as to scribe the arc. You can make a swift one-off trammel by running two screws, a set distance apart, through a length of thin wood.

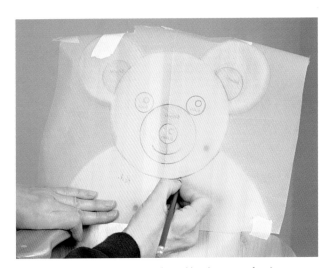

Use tracing paper to draw outlines like this. Transfer the outlines to the wood by flipping the paper over and tracing over the lines.

HAND TOOLS

Power-tool woodworkers also need a small range of traditional hand tools. The best advice is to start off with a basic kit consisting of the marking-out tools and one or two items like a saw, block plane and hammer, and then to buy specific tools if and when the need arises. Always buy the best tools that you can afford.

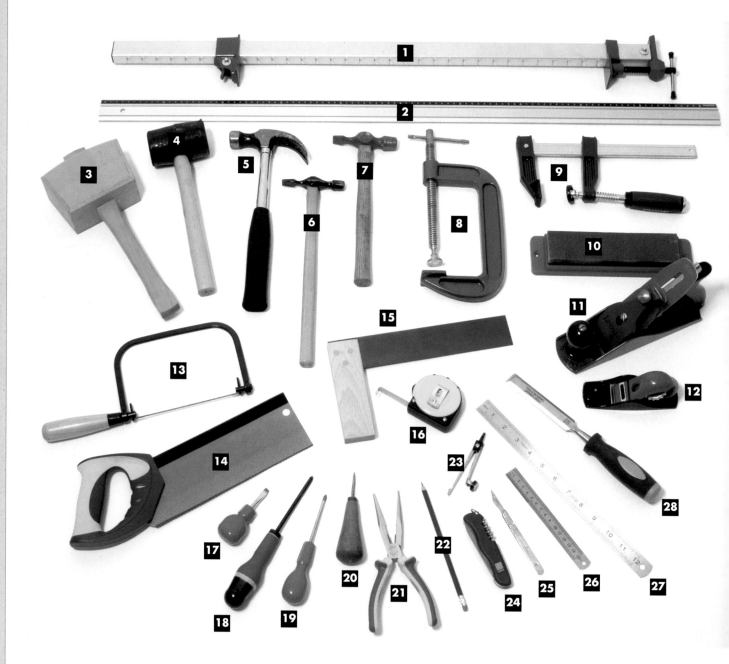

1 *Sash clamp* **2** *Ruler (1 m)* **3** *Mallet* **4** *Rubber mallet* **5** *Claw hammer* **6** *Lightweight pin hammer* **7** *Heavyweight pin hammer* **8** *G-clamp* **9** *Quick-release clamp* **10** *Combination oil stone* **11** *Smoothing plane* **12** *Block plane* **13** *Coping saw* **14** *Tenon saw* **15** *Try square* **16** *Tape measure* **17** *Short slot-head screwdriver* **18** *Medium crosshead screwdriver* **19** *Small crosshead screwdriver* **20** *Awl* **21** *Long-nose pliers* **22** *Pencil* **23** *Pair of compasses* **24** *Penknife* **25** *Scalpel* **26** *Ruler (150 mm/6 in)* **27** *Ruler (300 mm/12 in)* **28** *Bevel-edged chisel*

MARKING-OUT TOOLS

All woodwork starts with measurements and guidelines. You will need a tape measure, a ruler, a pencil, a try square for sorting out angles, a trammel or pair of compasses for drawing circles (see pages 22–23). An awl can be used for marking centre points for holes.

SAWS

Apart from the jigsaw and compound mitre saw already mentioned (see pages 20–21), you may need a tenon saw for cutting tenons and small sections of wood to length and for cutting large details, and a coping saw for small joints and curves. A general-purpose saw (panel saw) may be useful.

PLANES

Two planes are most useful – a smoothing plane for levelling and smoothing edges, and a block plane for levelling and smoothing end grain and for removing sharp corners on solid wood. Occasionally, you will need to sharpen a plane blade (see below).

CHISELS

You may need a set of chisels. A set of good-quality bevel-edged chisels is a good option – buy the best that you can afford. Chisels need sharpening frequently (see below).

SHARPENING STONE

Use a combination oil stone (coarse one side and fine on the other) or diamond stone to sharpen chisels and plane blades. Only use the coarse side if the blade is nicked or you wish to straighten the edge. Set the stone on the bench (a damp cloth will prevent it from slipping), squirt oil on the stone, put the bevel side of the tool next to the stone, hold the blade near to the cutting edge with the bevel flat on the stone and grind in a circular motion. For ordinary sharpening and after coarse grinding, use the fine side of the stone. Grind in the same way as described above and continue until a burred edge (feathered edge) appears. Turn the blade over (bevel side facing away from the stone) and lay it flat on the stone. Draw it towards you once to remove the burr.

HAMMERS AND MALLETS

Use a claw hammer for hefty nailing and for removing nails, and a pin hammer for small nailing and pinning tasks. When assembling furniture you may need a rubber mallet for striking the wood without denting it. Use a wooden mallet for hitting chisels when cutting joints.

KNIVES

I use a small penknife for sharpening pencils and for whittling little pegs and dowels.

CLAMPS

G-clamps are needed for holding the workpiece on the bench, for holding components together while you work, and for some gluing tasks. Quick-release clamps are similar to G-clamps but are quicker to adjust and are available in much larger sizes. Sash clamps are used for holding boards, frames or cabinet-type constructions while the glue dries. Corner clamps and strap clamps are worth buying if you intend to make lots of frames. Edging clamps are useful for fixing thin strips of wood to the edges of board (an alternative to pins). If you are keen on making jigs for producing components in batches, you are likely to need some special clamps that can be screwed to a baseboard and preset for quick operation.

DRILL BITS

You will need twist bits for holes less than 10 mm ($^{13}/_{32}$ in) in diameter and flat bits or forstner bits for larger holes. Forstner bits cut a flat-bottomed hole (flat bits have a very long brad point, a spike at the tip, and are therefore unsuitable for some jobs) but must be used in a pillar drill (not in a hand-held drill). Twist bits with brad points are more accurate in use. You may also need a counter-bore bit for making recessed screw holes (that are also suitable for receiving wooden plugs to conceal the screw head), a plug cutter to match the counter-bore, and a countersink for finishing holes before using countersink screws. Combination bits are available, which do more than one task/type of hole in one go (see page 36). For extra-large holes, consider using a hole saw.

MISCELLANEOUS TOOLS

As well as the woodworking tools, you may also need a small hacksaw for trimming up nails and for cutting metal rods to length, a file for smoothing the sawn edges, and pliers for any number of tasks. Long-nose pliers are useful for holding and straightening pins as you hammer them in.

SHAPING WOOD

A good part of the pleasure of power-tool woodwork has to do with the hands-on satisfaction of shaping the wood. The sight and sound of the tools, the smell of the wood and the great feeling of getting it right are all wonderfully enjoyable experiences, which should not be missed.

MARKING OUT

Take your carefully selected pieces of planed wood and sort them into groups. Mark each piece so that you know how it fits into the scheme of things, and use the pencil and ruler to set out the lengths. Take the square and run the marked points around the wood, so that you know which parts need to be cut away. Cutting lines can be scored with a knife. If the details are small, it helps to shade in the waste up to the cutting line, so that you know precisely where to run the saw cut. Use the compass to set out curves.

Often furniture designs require mirror-image components – a left side and a right side, for example – and a common mistake is to produce identical components.

CUTTING STRAIGHT LINES

To cut a straight line, you have many tools to choose from including a general-purpose hand saw, a jigsaw and a compound mitre saw. If you opt to use the jigsaw for producing accurate straight cuts, it is advisable to cut 1 mm ($\frac{1}{32}$ in) to the waste side of the drawn line, so that you can plane back to a perfect finish. A hand-held circular saw is good for cutting straight lines, especially in large boards, but we do not recommend using this tool unless you are an experienced woodworker.

CUTTING CURVED SHAPES

To cut a curve, you have a choice of using a jigsaw, a hand coping saw, a fret saw or an electric scroll saw. It is best to use a jigsaw for cutting large curves and a coping saw for smaller jobs. A fret saw and a scroll saw are useful for fine and intricate work.

To use a coping saw, adjust the tension until the blade 'pings' when plucked, set the workpiece on the worktable or in the vice, and work the saw with a rapid up-and-down action. If you see the blade wandering away from the drawn line, ease back and modify the direction of approach. To cut

A jigsaw is a general-purpose saw, which is ideal for cutting curves, straight lines and angled cuts. It is normally guided by hand and not with the use of a side fence.

out a 'window', drill a hole through the waste, unhitch the saw blade and pass it through the hole, then re-tension and make the cut as described above.

DRILLING HOLES

Use a small drill press in conjunction with a forstner bit for drilling holes greater than 10 mm ($\frac{13}{32}$ in) in diameter that need to be precisely placed. Establish the centre of the hole, fit the appropriate size of bit, set the depth stop, and clamp the workpiece securely to the worktable. Lower the bit to ensure that the centre point is directly on target, then switch on the power and run the hole through. For deep holes, lift the bit out several times to remove the waste and to minimize overheating. Always use clamps when you are using a large-diameter bit.

A power drill used with a twist bit is a good option when you want to drill holes for screws and perhaps pilot holes for nails. It is best to use a cordless drill, so that you don't have to worry about the cable snaking around the workshop. Switch on the power, set the point of the bit on the mark, make sightings to ensure that the bit is square to the face being drilled, then run the hole through. Use a screwdriver bit in a cordless driver when you are faced with the chore of putting in a lot of screws.

Hole saws (a cylinder-shaped saw blade) are used for producing large-diameter holes.

PLANING SURFACES

Rough-sawn planks need to be prepared using a surface planer (jointer) and a thicknesser (see page 19). If you just need to reduce the dimensions of a piece of ready-prepared wood, you can use a portable thicknesser, but these are expensive pieces of machinery. Hand-held power planers are available but we do not recommend using these unless you are an experienced woodworker.

A smoothing plane and a block plane are useful for finishing edges, reducing the width of a piece of wood by a few millimetres or so and for taking off sharp corners. Adjust the blade of a hand plane so that it takes the lightest of skimming cuts, carry out a trial on a piece of scrap wood first, then make the stroke.

ROUTING GROOVES, REBATES, PROFILES AND RECESSED AREAS

Though much depends upon the size, position and character of the groove, rebate, profile or recess to be worked, the basic procedure involves fitting the cutter, setting the depth

stop, and then lowering the plunge mechanism and running a groove or profile to the desired length. The accuracy of the cut relates to the setting of the fence, the speed of advance, and your eye–hand control. Make sure that you clear the waste after each pass to avoid overheating the bit.

Cutting an edge profile (a rounded edge for example) is one of the easiest routing procedures, especially if the cutter is fitted with a guide pin or bearing at the tip – no fence is required. Set the router on the edge of the workpiece (but keep the cutter away from the wood), switch it on, wait until it achieves full speed and then push or pull the tool up to and along the edge to make the cut. If you push away from your body, the workpiece must be on your left side, and if you are pulling towards yourself, the workpiece must be on your right side. The pin/bearing tip runs along the edge of the wood and controls the position of the router.

When routing, always consider the direction and the depth of the cut. Often, more than one pass will be necessary, with subsequent passes set to cut more deeply.

ROUTERS

Not so long ago, if you wanted to cut a groove, shape a fancy moulding, cut a rebate or cut a tongue and groove, you had no choice but to use a heap of chisels and various dedicated hand planes. The wonderful thing is that you can now do everything with a router.

Routing produces accurate results but half the work is in the setting up before the actual cutting takes place.

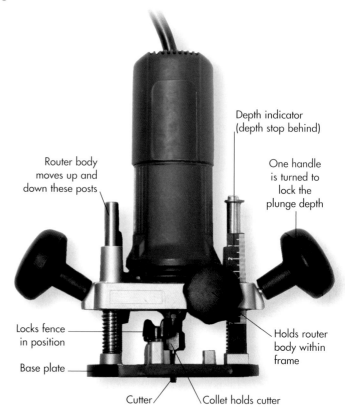

Depth indicator (depth stop behind)

Router body moves up and down these posts

One handle is turned to lock the plunge depth

Locks fence in position

Holds router body within frame

Base plate

Cutter

Collet holds cutter

Router

Novice woodworkers tend to be a bit intimidated by routers. Certainly they are noisy and dusty, and you do need to wear a dust mask, goggles and ear-defenders. They are not as much fun as using a plane, but they are swift and cost-efficient. A good-quality router and a selection of cutters are essential items for every woodworker.

A router is a drill-like tool. It is fitted with variously shaped and sized cutters, which are a reverse of the profile that you want to cut. For example, a chisel-shaped cutter will make a groove-shaped cut.

A router can be used in two ways. It can be held in the hand and run forward in much the same way as you might use a hand plane, or it can be upturned and fitted in a router table, so that it becomes a stationary bench machine; in the latter case, the wood is held and moved so that it comes into contact with the cutter.

HANDLES AND PLUNGE LOCK

Most routers have two handles, one fixed and the other in the form of a lock. You set the plunge lock handle to the required depth, hold both handles (one in each hand), bear down and push the router forward. The return springs counterbalance the weight of the motor, with the effect that, when you ease back on the handles and release the plunge lock, the cutter rises clear of the wood.

DEPTH STOP

The depth stop controls the total depth of the cut. You set the depth stop, say, to 12 mm ($1\frac{5}{32}$ in), and then make a series of deeper and deeper skimming passes until the desired depth is reached. You should probably be able to clear that depth with four passes, with each pass being 3 mm ($\frac{1}{8}$ in) deeper than the one before it.

FITTING CUTTERS

To fit a cutter, pull out the mains plug, lock the spindle with the lock button or pin, use the spanner to slacken the collet nut, insert your chosen cutter, tighten up the collet nut, and unlock the spindle. If a cutter is jammed, wiggle it loose or use a short stick to lever it free. Don't use a screwdriver or chisel, and be careful that you don't stress the router spindle, cut your fingers or break the cutter.

BASE PLATE AND GUIDE BUSH

The base plate is the foot or plate on which the frame, the motor, the side fence and so on are mounted. In some operations, when the base plate is used as a guide, the side of the plate is run against a straight-edge or jig. The guide bush is screwed to the underside of the base plate; it is used in situations when, although you want to use the router against a straight-edge or jig, the distance between the cutter and the edge of the base plate is too great.

SIDE FENCE

The side fence on a router is used in much the same way as the side fence on a power saw or rebate plane. If you are cutting a groove down a length of wood, say 25 mm ($^{31}/_{32}$ in) away from the edge, set the fence 25 mm ($^{31}/_{32}$ in) away from the cutter and run the router down the edge of the workpiece so that the fence is always in contact with the wood. If the wood is straight-edged and you make sure that the fence stays in contact, then the groove cannot be anything other than parallel to the edge of the workpiece.

HINTS AND TIPS

- Always follow the manufacturer's instructions.
- Always wear goggles and a dust mask.
- Make sure that the power is switched off when you are making adjustments to the router.
- Always make a trial cut to verify that your chosen cutter and setting are right for the task.
- Always make the cut with the wood to the left side of the tool.
- When you are routing, always move the router in the correct direction (see page 27).

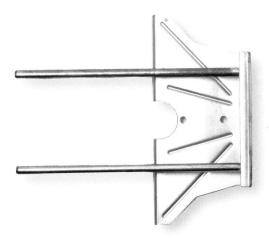

The side fence is an attachment that is always supplied with a router. It is used to produce cuts parallel to the edge of the wood.

A selection of router cutters for general work. **1** *Straight cutter for square-sided grooves and rebates* **2** *Straight cutter for narrow grooves* **3** *Round-over cutter with bearing tip for producing rounded edges* **4** *Radius cutter for making round-bottomed trenches* **5** *Flush-trimming cutter for trimming to an edge or template*

JOINTS

A good woodworking joint is a joy to the eye and a joy to the hand. One moment you have two quite separate pieces of wood, and the next you have a single unit, with the structure either perfectly concealed or perfectly decorative. Here, we will show you how to achieve all the joints used in this book.

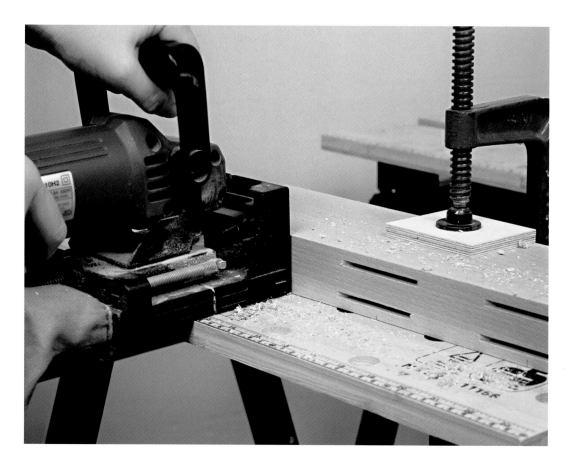

Biscuit jointing is a quick way to join boards edge to edge or at 90°. The biscuit jointer produces uniform saw cuts ready to receive 'biscuits' (see page 33).

BUTT JOINTS

Of all the joints, a butt joint is the simplest. In essence, it consists of two pieces of wood set one to another – edge to edge, end to end, edge to face, face to face, end to edge, and so on – with the two pieces meeting at right angles or at a mitred angle and fixed with pins, nails, dowels, biscuits and glue, or with a combination of these. With the strength of the joint coming from the quality of the contact (meaning the way the two pieces of wood meet), it is vital that the butting surfaces are prepared so that they come together for a smooth, clean, crisp fit.

The working procedure involves using a plane to trim the edges and faces until the two pieces look to be a perfect flush fit, and then holding them together and up to the light. If

you cannot see the light shining between the mating surfaces, it is a good fit. Finally, the mating surfaces are spread with glue and fixed with pins and/or screws. You can increase the strength by backing the joint with additional members, such as blocks or screwed battens.

BISCUIT JOINTS

A biscuit joint works in much the same way as a tongue-and-groove joint (see opposite) or even a dowel joint (see page 32). Instead of having dowels that fit into holes, or a continuous tongue that fits in a continuous groove, however, flat, oval 'biscuits' of compressed beech (they get their name because they look just like thin oatmeal biscuits) are fitted into purpose-made slots.

A biscuit jointer is used to cut a pattern of slots in the prepared butt-jointed members. You then dribble glue into the slots, push biscuits into the slots, and clamp the members together. Although the technique is much the same as jointing with dowels, the cutting procedure allows for a good amount of adjustment. It is a good joint for beginners to make.

TONGUE-AND-GROOVE JOINTS

A tongue-and-groove joint is a wonderfully simple and useful structure. Although there are many variations on the theme, the basic joint involves cutting two pieces of wood so that there is a projection or tongue on one piece, which fits into a slot or groove on the other. Alternatively, the joint can be made so that both pieces of wood are grooved and then fitted together with a loose tongue. While the joint can be used in many edge-to-edge situations, tongue-and-groove joints are most often found in ready-made boarding, such as for the dog kennel (see page 126).

The joint is a good option when you want to clad a frame. In this instance, the tongue is slightly feathered, the face beaded and the whole thing fitted with cross-battens. The resultant joint is loosely fitted and decorative. While neighbouring boards can move, expand and shrink, according to environmental conditions, the tongue-and-groove structure continues to stop light and the passage of air, dust, and so on. In this context, it was and is used in situations where you might now also use inexpensive sheeting – for example, on the back of a cupboard or at the bottom of a drawer.

If you want to take the joint one step further – and this only works on boards that are thicker than 12 mm (^{15}⁄$_{32}$ in) – you can cut and work the tongue and groove for a tight, crisp, square-edged fit, and glue and clamp the boards together. The edges must be square and true, as with a butted joint.

REBATE JOINTS

The rebate joint, sometimes called a lap joint, is a basic corner joint used in box construction. The design involves bringing two component parts together in such a way that the end or edge of one part sits in the rebate or step of another. While this joint is not particularly strong or decorative, it is better than a butt joint, in that the wood remaining after the rebate has been cut forms a lap that covers the end grain of the part sitting in the rebate.

Tongue-and-groove joints are an effective and decorative way to join narrow boards and at the same time make allowances for wood movement.

In the context of this book, the joint is cut using a router. The router is fitted with a straight cutter and the fence, then the rebate is worked by running the fence hard up against the edge of the workpiece.

HOUSING JOINTS

The housing joint is a basic joint used in box and furniture construction. The design involves cutting a channel, trench, or housing across the grain in one piece, which is then used to receive or house the end or edge of another piece. (Note that, although grooves and housings are both channels, a groove is a channel that runs in the direction of the grain, while a housing is a channel that runs across the grain.) A housing is a really good option when you want to join, for example, the end of a shelf or divider so that it meets one or other of the side, top or bottom boards that go to make up a box or cabinet.

For the projects in this book, housings are best cut with a router. To do this, fit the router with a cutter that is the same width as (or narrower than) the housing channel you want to cut. Clamp a guide batten in place across the workpiece, and cut the housing by running the edge of the router's base plate hard up against the edge of the batten. If the cutter is the same width as the housing, it can be worked in one or more passes along the same track; if it is narrower, the full width of the housing is achieved by moving the guide batten and cutting a second channel alongside the first.

MORTISE-AND-TENON JOINTS

The mortise-and-tenon joint involves cutting a projecting tongue or tenon on the end of one piece so that it fits in a hole or mortise in another piece. The length, height and thickness of the tenon are determined by the design of the joint and the dimensions of the mortise member.

In the context of this book, the joint is best cut with a router and a chisel. The mortise is worked with a straight cutter in the router, in much the same way that you might cut a straight stopped groove. The dimensions are marked out and the hole is worked by making a series of side-by-side plunging cuts. A series of deeper and deeper cuts is made until the full depth is achieved, then tidied up with the chisel. The matching tenon is worked by cutting a step on the end of the member to be jointed, in much the same way as you might cut a rebate. You simply cut a long rebate on one face

of the tenon member, and then turn it over and repeat the procedure on the other face.

DOWEL JOINTS

A dowel joint involves first cutting a butt joint and then linking the two members with special fluted dowels, with the diameter, depth and number of dowels relating to the dimensions of the members being jointed.

For most projects, the holes are cut with the drill, with location of holes being achieved by means of a simple home-made jig. Set the jig in place on the prepared workpiece, drill the pattern of holes, and then glue and fit the dowels. Clamps are needed to hold the pieces together until the glue dries.

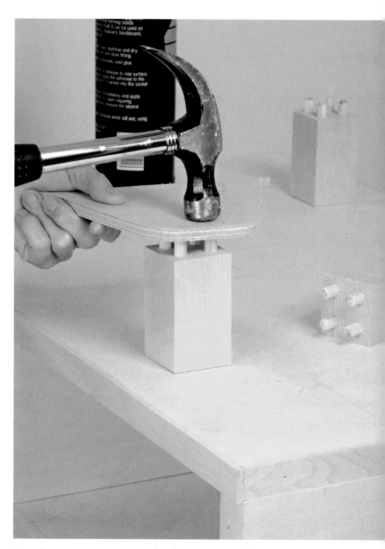

Dowel joints are easier to make than mortise-and-tenon joints but need to be marked and drilled as accurately as possible. Special fluted dowels are used.

BISCUIT JOINTERS

A biscuit jointer is the perfect power tool for newcomers to woodwork – it cuts accurate joints with the minimum of measuring and marking required. If you simply want to join two pieces of wood in the shortest space of time, this is the perfect tool. It also cuts grooves.

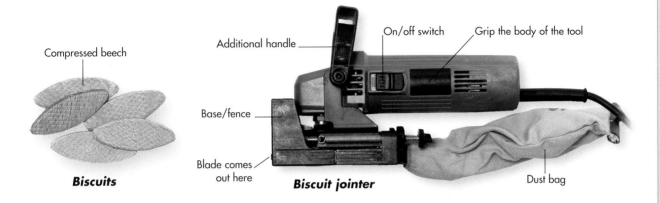

Compressed beech

Biscuits

Additional handle

On/off switch

Grip the body of the tool

Base/fence

Blade comes out here

Biscuit jointer

Dust bag

BISCUIT JOINTER FACTS

A biscuit joint works in much the same way as a dowel joint, but instead of fitting dowels in holes you fit flat, oval biscuits of compressed hardwood (beech is always used) into slots. The jointer is no more than a miniature circular saw fitted with various guards, guides and fences. Align the component parts that you want to join, set the jointer in place, cut matching slots in the two parts that need to be joined, then set the biscuits in the glued slots and clamp up.

DEPTH OF CUT

The depth of cut relates to the size of biscuit. Set the depth stop – say to 12 mm ($^{15}/_{32}$ in) – and then set the jointer in place and press down on the spring-loaded housing.

CENTRE-LINE ALIGNMENT

The centre-line mark on the base or fence indicates the centre of the slot – the widest part of the biscuit.

BLADES

A blade 100–105 mm ($3^{15}/_{16}$–$4^{1}/_{8}$ in) in diameter cuts a slot 4 mm ($^{5}/_{32}$ in) wide.

BISCUITS

Though compressed beech biscuits are sold in various sizes to suit the thickness of boards, a useful standard size is a number 20.

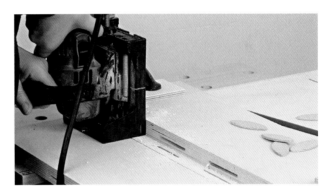

When jointing two pieces at 90°, clamp the pieces next to each other as shown (spaced apart by the thickness of the material).

HINTS AND TIPS

- Always wear goggles and a dust mask.
- Always follow the manufacturer's instructions.
- When making adjustments to the saw, make sure the power is switched off.
- If you are totally unfamiliar with the tool, have a trial run; cut slots of various depths and experiment with the biscuit sizes.
- Wait for the blade to reach full speed before making a plunge.
- Dribble PVA glue into the slot – not over the biscuit.

FIXINGS AND FITTINGS

There are hundreds of fixings and fittings on the market, many designed for very specific applications.
They are all good. The trick is choosing the one that is most appropriate for the task in hand.
The following listing shows you just a few of the exciting options.

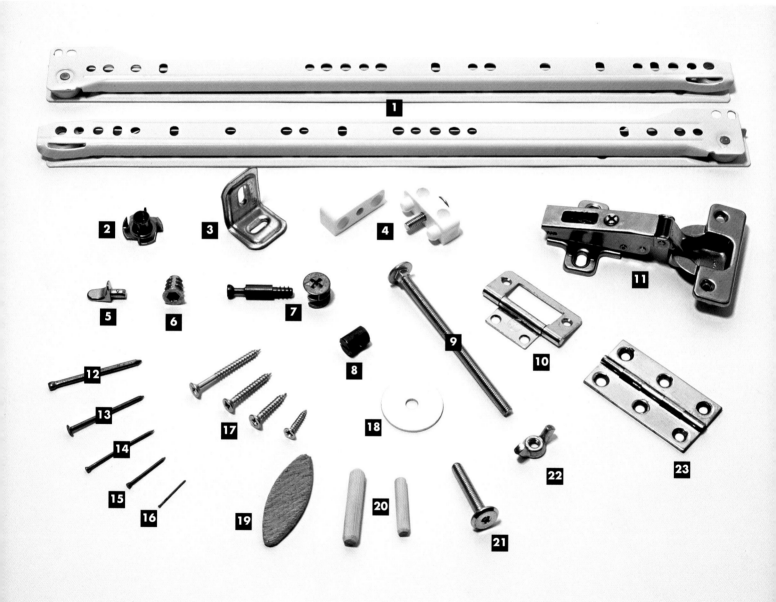

1 Drawer runners (pair) **2** Pronged T-nut **3** Shrinkage plate **4** Plastic block knock-down fixing **5** Shelf support **6** Threaded insert
7 Cam dowel fixing **8** Threaded cross-dowel **9** Coach bolt **10** No-mortise hinge **11** European-style concealed hinge
12 Oval-headed nail **13** Flat-headed nail, **14–16** Pins **17** Crossheaded screws **18** Washer **19** Biscuit
20 Fluted dowels **21** Socket screw **22** Wing nut **23** Butt hinge

SCREWS

There are slotted, crossheaded, steel, brass and plated screws, in just about every size, shape and design that you can imagine. Always choose a screw that is about three times as long as the thickness of wood to be fixed, but not so long that it breaks through the other component. If you have a power screwdriver, crossheaded screws are a good option.

Use a cordless driver and crossheaded screws for the projects in this book.

NAILS AND PINS

There are round wire nails with flat heads, oval-headed nails, lost-headed nails, panel pins, and others too numerous to mention. Flat heads are good when you don't mind having the heads on show, and lost heads are ideal when you want to make the head 'disappear' below the surface of the wood.

HINGES

Apart from the traditional brass and steel butt hinges that most people recognize – on room doors and cupboards – there are now hinges that are designed variously to be used with sheet wood, to be fitted by means of drilling holes, that have spring-loaded closing mechanisms, and so on.

BLOCK JOINTS

The block joint consists of two plastic blocks that fit together, a bit like children's plastic building bricks. You screw one block to each component part, then draw the two together by means of an integral clamping bolt. They are a great option when you want to join large sheets of plywood and suchlike.

Use cam dowel fixings for knock-down furniture.

CAM DOWELS

Cam dowels are ingenious. They consist of two metal components: a screw dowel and a circular cam. You screw the dowel into one part, drill a hole and fit the cam into the other part; then you slide the two parts together until the peg locates. Rotating the cam locks the parts together.

SHRINKAGE PLATES

These are right-angled metal plates that are designed to be used in situations when you want to join one part to another, yet at the same time allow for the shrinkage of the timber. The slots allow the wood to move.

DRAWER RUNNERS

These are useful steel and nylon runners designed for knock-down-type cabinets. You screw one part to the frame and the other to the drawer. The little wheels on the drawer part fit into the track on the other part in such a way that the drawer runs very smoothly.

Metal runners are the quickest solution for drawers.

DRILLS AND DRIVERS

Of all the power tools, the two most popular items are the mains-powered drill and the cordless drill-driver (known as a cordless driver). Not long ago cordless drivers were expensive and rather disappointing because they did not quite have the power to do the job, but they are now very efficient low-cost tools.

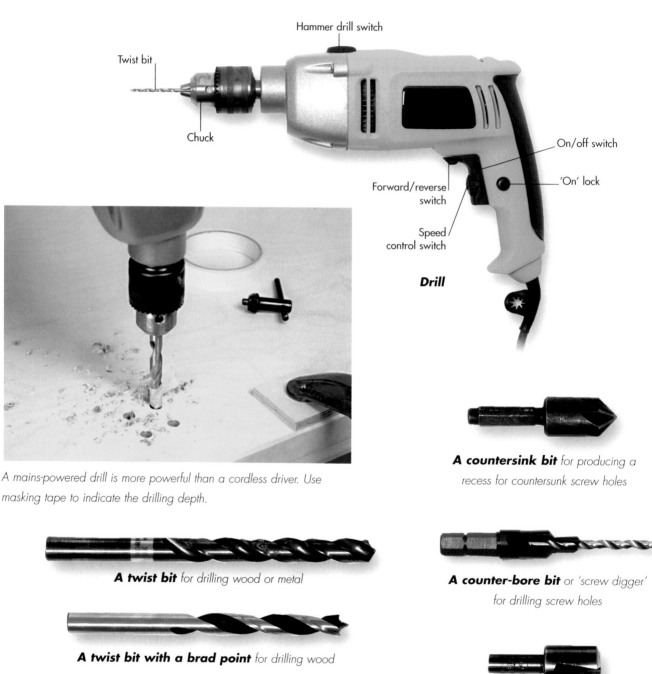

Hammer drill switch

Twist bit

Chuck

On/off switch

Forward/reverse switch

'On' lock

Speed control switch

Drill

A mains-powered drill is more powerful than a cordless driver. Use masking tape to indicate the drilling depth.

A countersink bit for producing a recess for countersunk screw holes

A twist bit for drilling wood or metal

A twist bit with a brad point for drilling wood

A flat bit for large-diameter holes in wood

A counter-bore bit or 'screw digger' for drilling screw holes

A plug cutter for making solid wood plugs that fit in a counter-bored hole

Keyless chuck
Torque control
Speed switch
On/off switch
Forward/reverse switch
Rechargeable battery

Cordless driver

A combination screwdriver bit
for inserting crossheaded screws

A magnetic bit holder *for quick changing of screwdriver bits*

A combination bit *for drilling screw holes incorporating a countersink*

MAINS-POWERED DRILL AND CORDLESS DRIVER FACTS

While mains-powered drills are only used for drilling holes, cordless drivers are used both for drilling holes and for driving in screws. Cordless options are now so good that for the most part they can be used for all the drilling and driving tasks employed in woodworking. My advice is to get the biggest and best cordless driver that you can afford, and see how it goes. You might never need to get a mains drill.

CHUCK CAPACITY

The size of the chuck decides the maximum drill bit size. A 13 mm (½ in) keyless chuck is a good option, but 10 mm (13⁄32 in) is more common.

KEYLESS CHUCKS

A fast-action keyless chuck allows you both to fit and to remove a drill bit without the need for a chuck key – a really good option if you are untidy.

REVERSE ACTION

A reverse-action capability allows you to change the direction of spin. This is useful when you are removing lots of screws.

CHARGING

Cordless drivers have a rechargeable battery that fixes to the handle. A second battery is a good investment.

TORQUE CONTROL

This function sets the driver to stop driving once a preset torque has been applied. This can be used to prevent you driving the screws too far into the wood.

HINTS AND TIPS

- Always follow the manufacturer's instructions.
- When you are making adjustments to the drill, make sure the power is switched off.
- Cordless drivers are much easier to use with crossheaded screws.
- Make sure that the point of the screwdriver is well located before switching on the power.
- A variable speed is good when driving in screws, as it allows you to exert maximum control.

FINISHING

Finishing is the act of sanding, texturing, painting, waxing, oiling or otherwise enhancing the appearance of a piece of woodwork. The object of the exercise is to protect the wood, and in so doing, to create an easy-to-clean finish that looks and feels good.

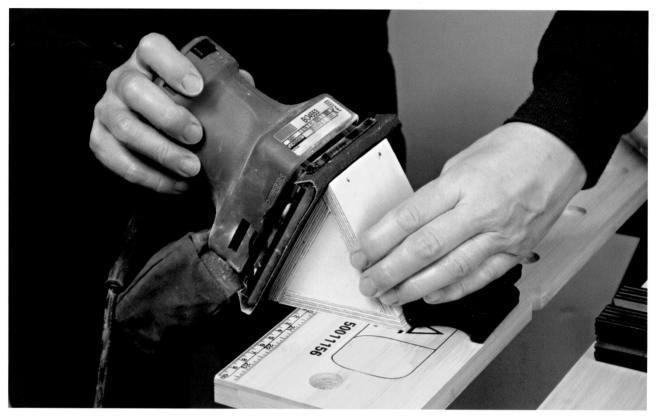

A palm sander is a small orbital sander. It is convenient to use when sanding small areas and when rounding over edges.

SANDING

The sanding procedure involves using different grades of sandpaper to produce a smooth finish. You can sand by hand, holding the paper as a folded sheet or wrapped around a block, or you can use an electric sander.

It is useful to have an orbital sander and a palm sander, which is smaller. Most orbital sanders use a third of a sheet of sandpaper, but palm sanders use a quarter of a sheet. Sandpaper can be bought more cheaply by the roll from specialist suppliers. Sanders that only use special, uniquely shaped sanding sheets are an expensive option and one to avoid. Belt sanders are the most powerful but are difficult to control. Use 80-grit sandpaper for initial smoothing and rounding over of edges and 600-grit sandpaper for finishing.

NATURAL FINISHES

Although the literal meaning of a natural finish is that the wood is sanded and then left in its natural state, the term has also come to mean a surface that has been oiled or waxed. Danish oil and teak oil can be applied with a cotton cloth or a brush. All you do is lay on a thin coat, let it dry, wipe it over with the finest sandpaper and then apply another thin coat. If you want to soften the surface, you can follow the second rubbing-down with wax polish.

For projects that come into direct contact with food, such as the chopping board (see page 52), use ordinary olive oil wiped on with a cloth.

Varnish-type finishes are difficult to apply, and you may therefore wish to avoid them.

An orbital sander is far quicker than sanding by hand, and is easy to use. Apply even pressure and move back and forth continuously in the direction of the grain.

PAINTED FINISH

When it comes to painting a finished project, you have a choice between using spirit-based oil paint or water-based acrylic paint. Both paints need to be carefully applied with a brush. Although there are now flat and shiny options in both types of paint, the main difference is that oil paintbrushes need to be cleaned with white spirit, while the acrylic brushes can be cleaned under running water. It is a matter of personal choice as to which you prefer. Currently, I choose paints for their depth and quality of colour. As to the toxic effects, oil fumes can make you drowsy, while acrylic fumes may dry your throat. Wear a mask to protect you from toxic vapours, and as far as possible, do the painting out in the open.

Paint washes, as with the sun lounger project (see page 120), can be very attractive. To create a wash, you simply decant some of your chosen paint and mix it with the appropriate thinner – water or white spirit – until you have a thin, watery wash that looks about right for your needs.

Some sanding jobs are best done by hand. Fiddly areas like this handle hole need to be smooth and round-edged. Use sandpaper wrapped around a dowel.

SANDERS

A power sander is a must – after all, it takes the sweat out of what is essentially a very tedious task. You will still need to do a bit of hand sanding to remove deep scratches and to get into small areas, but a well-chosen orbital sander will ensure that hand sanding is kept to a minimum.

SANDER FACTS

There are belt sanders, sanders with fancy rubber heads, small sanders that just about fit in the palm of one hand, little sanders with pointed heads that are used to getting into difficult corners, the basic orbital sander, and all manner of variations in between. It is best to start by getting a good-quality orbital sander, and then worry about other types if and when the need arises.

SANDING SHEETS

Sanding sheets are sold according to grit size, sheet size and sheet shape. A typical range of sanding sheet grades runs from very coarse through to coarse, medium, fine, very fine and superfine. If you are looking for the cheapest option, avoid sanders that need to be fitted with very specific self-adhesive sanding sheets, and choose an orbital sander that is designed to take a third of a sheet of standard-size sandpaper. All you do is tear the standard sheet into three equal pieces, fit one piece in the sander, and you are ready to go.

DUST EXTRACTION

There are three ways of dealing with wood dust. You can fit your chosen sander with a dust bag, you can have a large dust extractor that fits the duct at the back of the sander, and you can wear a dust mask. Of course, the best option is to have all three systems up and running, but a good middle way is to fit the dust bag, wear a mask, and use a vacuum cleaner to clear up the mess at the end of the day.

DISC SANDERS

Disc sanders have been around for a long time, and they are low in cost, but they tend to leave such deep directional scratches that they are unsuitable for most woodwork.

Orbital sander

On/off switch
'On' lock
Connection for dust collection
Holds sandpaper in position
⅓ of a sheet of sandpaper

Palm sander

On/off switch
Holds sandpaper in position
Connection for dust collection
¼ of a sheet of sandpaper

HINTS AND TIPS

- Always follow the manufacturer's instructions.

- Always wear goggles and a dust mask.

- When you are making adjustments to the sander, make sure that the power is switched off.

- Avoid so-called 'finishing sanders' that need to be fitted with specially shaped sanding profiles – they are expensive, and will not produce a ready-to-finish surface.

- Orbital sanders are the best option, in that the movement results in a semi-random sanding pattern that is virtually scratch-free. It is not as good as sanding by hand, but it is the next best thing.

OTHER USEFUL POWER TOOLS

Woodworking is a wonderful activity, but only if you are using the right tool for the task. It is no good battling with the wrong saw or drill, and then thinking that woodworking is not for you. You need to choose your tools with care. The following list describes a few more options.

SPECIAL MACHINES

There are lots of woodworking power tools and machines on the market, everything from joint cutters, spindle moulders and tenon cutters through to lathes, and many others besides. What happens in the normal course of events is that the novice woodworker very soon develops an expertise in a particular area and then buys the appropriate tool or small machine to suit. For example, if you become interested in joint-making, you might buy a dedicated mortiser, then perhaps a jig for cutting dovetails, then a special machine to hone your chisels, and so on.

After you have followed through the projects in this book – buying one or two basic tools, but otherwise generally begging and borrowing along the way – you will better understand your particular needs and interests, and can then decide to invest in other tools.

CIRCULAR SAW TABLE

A circular saw is a machine for sawing stock to width and length. In essence, there is a table with a circular saw blade at the centre, with a rip fence to the right side and a sliding table to the left. You set the rip fence to the desired width, then use your hands and a push stick to move the wood through. It is a good machine for converting wide boards and for slicing up sheet material.

PLANER-THICKNESSER

A planer-thicknesser is a combination machine that is designed to plane all sides and edges of the wood square to each other. You first plane one face, then one edge, then the other face, and finally the other edge. Professional woodworkers generally use two machines – a surface planer and a thicknesser – but home woodworkers tend to opt for a dual purpose planer-thicknesser.

BAND SAW

An electric band saw is a bench machine made up of a flexible looped blade running over and being driven by two or more wheels. It is designed for cutting broad curves in any thickness of wood. Narrow blades suit tight curves, while wide blades are better for broad curves in thick wood. I use a small, two-wheeled machine fitted with a 6 mm ($\frac{1}{4}$ in) blade.

DRILL PRESS

The drill press (sometimes also called the bench drill or pillar drill) is a machine that is dedicated to drilling holes. While you might think that a small, hand-held power drill is sufficient, a good-sized drill press is a winner, in that it enables you to bore accurately placed holes every time. You fit the bit in the chuck, clamp the workpiece to the workbench, set the depth gauge, then pull the capstan wheel to bore out the hole. A drill press teamed up with forstner drill bits is an excellent combination. There are some very good inexpensive machines on the market.

SCROLL SAW

The scroll saw is a fine-bladed saw designed for cutting intricate curves in thin-section wood. The blade is tensioned, then the workpiece is fed towards the blade. With blade-changing being an ongoing event – almost at the start of every new project – the best machines are fitted with large, easy-to-turn thumbscrews. To saw out a 'window' in the middle of a piece of wood, detach one end of the blade and pass it through a drilled hole.

RADIAL ARM SAW

The radial arm saw is one step up from the compound mitre saw (but similar to a sliding compound mitre saw). The blade slides and therefore cuts across wider boards and is useful for making grooves, rebates, housings and tenons. It is an expensive tool but a good option for a keen home woodworker as it is compact and versatile. To use the machine, clamp the workpiece on the workbench, set the blade at the appropriate bevel, swing the head of the machine around to the desired angle, set the depth of cut, then switch on the power and make the cut.

PROJECTS

Now is the time to get down to the wonderfully exciting business of building the various projects. Don't worry if you are a beginner: the book will take you gently through all the stages. This is not one of those books where the projects are so boringly easy that they are not worth doing. Every project will, in one way or another, present you with a good, solid challenge.

Enough … no more praise and promise, no more talking about it. Now is the time to roll up your sleeves and experience the truly joyous, finger-tingling pleasures of working with wood!

All projects require the following basic equipment: a portable workbench (sometimes two are better if the items are large), pencil, tape measure, ruler and a try square.

COFFEE TABLE

When we designed this particular piece, we thought of it as being a coffee table, with baskets underneath for storing magazines. Then, when friends and family congratulated us on our beautiful 'TV and video' table, it occurred to us that it could be used for just that purpose. The dimensions might have to be changed to suit the size of the various pieces of equipment, and you would need to leave out the baskets, but it would certainly do the job. The moral of this tale is that you must be prepared to change things around to suit your own needs. If you like our design complete with the baskets, start by getting your baskets and then tweak the measurements to suit.

YOU WILL NEED

- Jigsaw

- Compound mitre saw

- Biscuit jointer with 24 x No. 20 biscuits

- Drill and 10 mm (¹³⁄₃₂ in) twist bit with a brad point

- Cordless driver and screwdriver bit to fit your screws

- Orbital sander, 80-grit and 600-grit sandpaper

- Claw hammer and pin hammer

- Nail punch

- 2 G-clamps and 2 sash clamps

- Birch plywood:
  A 3 pieces, 822 x 510 x 24 mm (32⅜ x 20⅛₂ x 1 in)
  B 3 pieces, 510 x 152 x 24 mm (20³⁄₃₂ x 5³¹⁄₃₂ x 1 in)

- Maple:
  C 4 pieces, 88 x 50 x 50 mm (3¹⁵⁄₃₂ x 1³¹⁄₃₂ x 1³¹⁄₃₂ in)
  D 6 pieces, 832 x 24 x 5 mm (32²⁵⁄₃₂ x 1 x ³⁄₁₆ in)
  E 6 pieces, 510 x 24 x 5 mm (20³⁄₃₂ x 1 x ³⁄₁₆ in)
  F 6 pieces, 152 x 24 x 5 mm (5³¹⁄₃₂ x 1 x ³⁄₁₆ in)

- Fluted dowels: 32 x 10 mm (¹³⁄₃₂ in) in diameter, 40 mm (1⁹⁄₁₆ in) long

- Veneer pins

- 4 swivelling castors with wheels 70 mm (2¾ in) in diameter and 20 mm (²⁵⁄₃₂ in) screws to suit

- Wood-coloured filler

- PVA glue

- Finishing oil

- Cloths for wiping up excess glue and applying oil

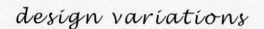

design variations

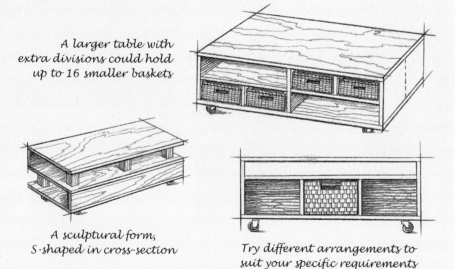

A larger table with extra divisions could hold up to 16 smaller baskets

A sculptural form, S-shaped in cross-section

Try different arrangements to suit your specific requirements

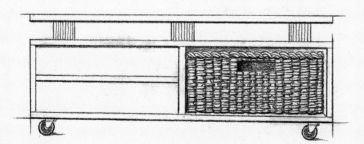

A non-symmetrical design might be more to your liking

Construction time: 2 weekends

Power tools required: biscuit jointer, jigsaw, compound mitre saw, drill, cordless driver and orbital sander

COFFEE TABLE CONSTRUCTION DRAWING

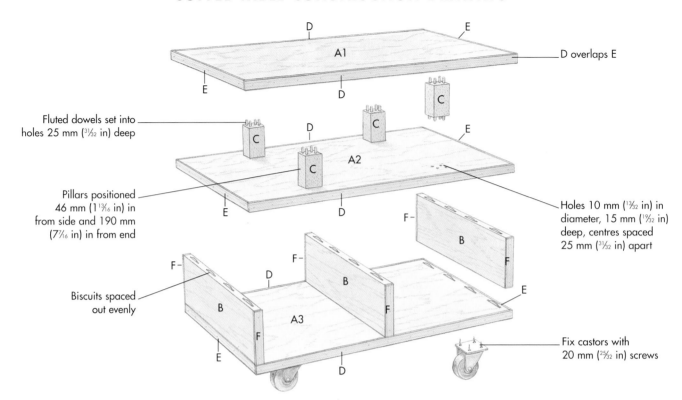

Fluted dowels set into holes 25 mm ($3\frac{1}{32}$ in) deep

Pillars positioned 46 mm ($1\frac{13}{16}$ in) in from side and 190 mm ($7\frac{7}{16}$ in) in from end

D overlaps E

Holes 10 mm ($1\frac{3}{32}$ in) in diameter, 15 mm ($1\frac{9}{32}$ in) deep, centres spaced 25 mm ($3\frac{1}{32}$ in) apart

Biscuits spaced out evenly

Fix castors with 20 mm ($2\frac{5}{32}$ in) screws

HOW TO BUILD THE COFFEE TABLE

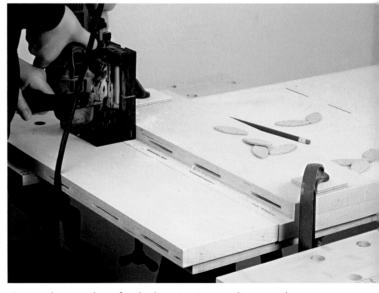

1 Cut out the main boards (A, B) from a sheet of birch plywood. Use glue, the pin hammer and veneer pins to fix the maple strips D, E and F to all four edges of the plywood. Knock the pinheads below the surface of the wood using the nail punch, wipe off excess glue with a damp cloth and fill the holes with wood-coloured filler.

2 Mark centre lines for the biscuit joints on the vertical boards (B). Place a vertical board on top of the adjoining horizontal board (A3) and clamp both to the workbench. Cut all the biscuit joints (see Biscuit jointers, page 33). Join the boards together using glue and sash clamps.

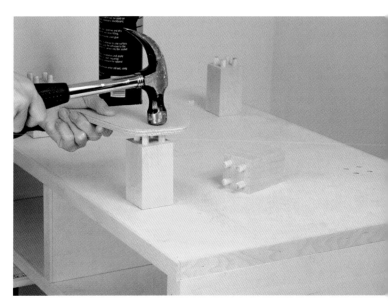

3 Allow the glue to dry overnight and remove the clamps. Use the pencil and ruler to mark in the position of the dowel holes. Wrap masking tape around the drill bit for a depth guide, and drill the holes. Cut the pillars (C) and drill dowel holes in the end. Do a trial assembly in order to check that the dowel holes are accurately placed.

4 Spread glue inside the holes in the ends of the pillars (C) and knock in the fluted dowels. Spread glue inside the holes in the boards (A1 and A2) and position the pillars. Use a hammer and a scrap of wood to knock them into place. Set the top surface in position, knock it down and clamp the joints with the sash clamps.

TIPS AND TROUBLESHOOTING

Edge strips We have described how to use edge strips that are exactly the same width as the thickness of the boards (this is the quickest way). You may prefer to use slightly wider strips and trim them flush using a router (see page 28).

Biscuit joints It is a good idea to test the depth of the cut on a scrap of wood before you proceed. Avoid a cut that is too shallow as this will prevent the joint from closing up fully.

Dowel joints The positions of the holes need to be marked out as accurately as possible with a sharp pencil. If the holes are misaligned or not vertical, the joint may not work. 'Dowel centres' (metal locators with centre points) can be used to mark corresponding holes accurately. A brad-point drill bit (with a spiked end) is far better than an ordinary twist bit.

5 Fix the swivelling castors near to the corners of the underside of the table (but not so near that the wheel sticks out awkwardly when it swivels). Round over any sharp edges with sandpaper and smooth all surfaces with the orbital sander. Wipe away the dust and apply the finishing oil (see page 38).

BATHROOM MIRROR CABINET

Our son had the problem of how to fit both a good-sized mirror and a cabinet into his amazingly small bathroom. He did not want the usual small, medicine-type cupboard with a mirror stuck on the front; the mirror would be too small and the storage space too poky, and he thought the design too old-fashioned. He wanted something a bit more generous and modern. After a lot of thought, it came to us that the best solution was to shift the emphasis, and have a mirror with storage, rather than storage with a mirror tacked on. So this design was born. While we like the simple arrangement with the two drawers underneath, if you look at the design variations you will see that you can easily change the arrangement to suit your needs.

YOU WILL NEED

- Jigsaw

- Compound mitre saw

- Biscuit jointer and 20 x No. 20 biscuits

- Router with a 12 mm (¹⁵⁄₃₂ in) straight cutter

- Orbital sander, 80-grit and 600-grit sandpaper

- Pin hammer

- 2 G-clamps and 2 sash clamps

- Pine:
  A 2 pieces, 726 x 142 x 18 mm (28¹⁹⁄₃₂ x 5¹⁹⁄₃₂ x ²³⁄₃₂ in)
  B 3 pieces, 600 x 142 x 18 mm (23⅝ x 5¹⁹⁄₃₂ x ²³⁄₃₂ in)
  C 2 pieces, 298 x 70 x 18 mm (11²³⁄₃₂ x 2¾ x ²³⁄₃₂ in)
  D 2 pieces, 262 x 70 x 18 mm (10⁵⁄₁₆ x 2¾ x ²³⁄₃₂ in)
  E 4 pieces, 105 x 70 x 18 mm (4⅛ x 2¾ x ²³⁄₃₂ in)

- Birch plywood:
  F 2 pieces, 270 x 95 x 4 mm (10⅝ x 3¾ x ⁵⁄₃₂ in)
  G 1 piece, 612 x 84 x 6 mm (27³⁄₃₂ x 3⁵⁄₁₆ x ¼ in)
  H 2 pieces, 100 x 100 x 4 mm (3¹⁵⁄₁₆ x 3¹⁵⁄₁₆ x ⁵⁄₃₂ in)

- Mirror glass:
  I 1 piece, 612 x 612 x 6 mm (27³⁄₃₂ x 27³⁄₃₂ x ¼ in)

- Pins: 20 mm (²⁵⁄₃₂ in) long

- PVA glue

- Finishing oil

- Cloths for wiping up excess glue and applying oil

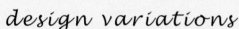

design variations

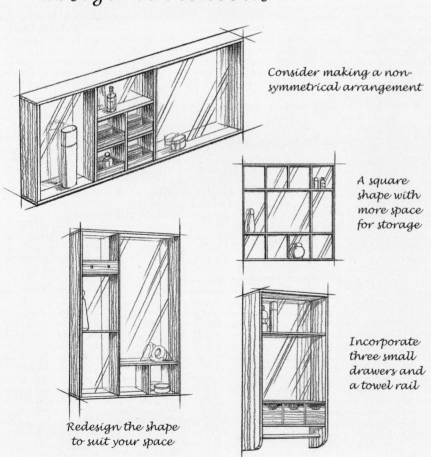

Consider making a non-symmetrical arrangement

A square shape with more space for storage

Incorporate three small drawers and a towel rail

Redesign the shape to suit your space

Construction time: 1 weekend

Power tools required: router, biscuit jointer, jigsaw, compound mitre saw and orbital sander

BATHROOM MIRROR CABINET CONSTRUCTION DRAWING

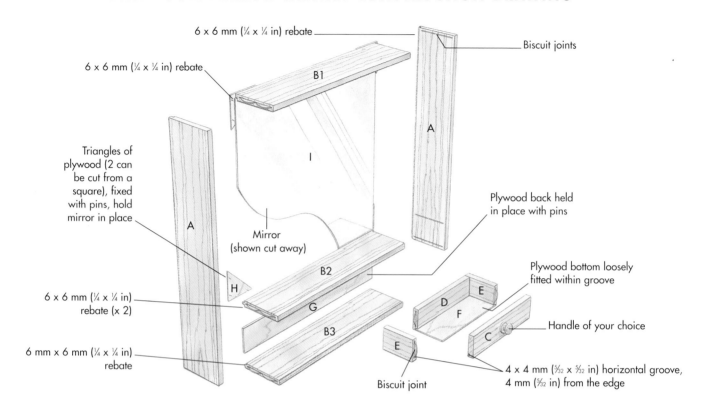

6 x 6 mm (¼ x ¼ in) rebate

6 x 6 mm (¼ x ¼ in) rebate

Biscuit joints

B1

A

Triangles of plywood (2 can be cut from a square), fixed with pins, hold mirror in place

A

I

Plywood back held in place with pins

Mirror (shown cut away)

Plywood bottom loosely fitted within groove

B2

H

D   E

6 x 6 mm (¼ x ¼ in) rebate (x 2)

G

F

Handle of your choice

B3

E

C

6 mm x 6 mm (¼ x ¼ in) rebate

E

4 x 4 mm (⁵⁄₃₂ x ⁵⁄₃₂ in) horizontal groove, 4 mm (⁵⁄₃₂ in) from the edge

Biscuit joint

HOW TO BUILD THE BATHROOM MIRROR CABINET

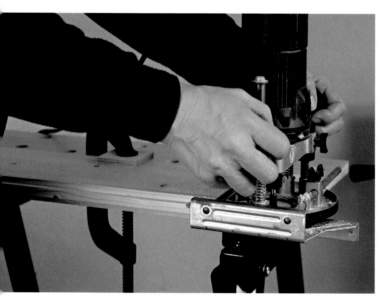

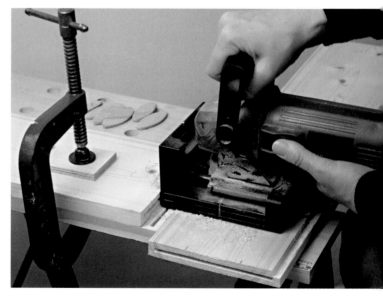

1 Use a pencil, tape measure and ruler to draw out on the wood the shapes of the boards (A, B) that make the frame. Fit the router with the fence and straight cutter, and – one board at a time – hold the router against the edge to be worked, and cut the rebates (B2 has two rebates).

2 Use a pencil and ruler to mark in the position of the paired biscuit slots on the five boards A and B, which make the overall mirror frame. Clamp a pair of butting boards in place, switch on the power, align the jointer with the marks, and cut the slots.

3 Perform a dry trial run to make sure that everything fits and comes together properly, then dribble a small amount of PVA glue into the slots and tap the biscuits home. When you are happy with the placing of the biscuits, assemble the frame and clamp up. When the glue is dry, fix the plywood back (G) in position using pins.

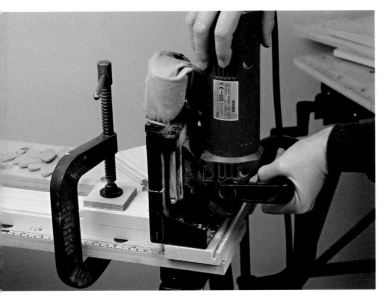

5 Mark the paired biscuit slots on the drawers (C, D, E). Clamp a pair of butting boards to the bench, align the jointer with the marks, and cut the slots. Glue and fit the biscuits, insert the drawer bottoms (F) and clamp up. Sand and apply the oil. Position the mirror (I) and pin a triangle of plywood (H) at each corner.

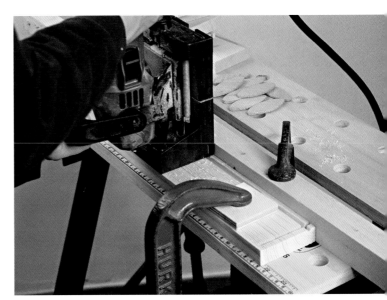

4 Take the drawer sides (C, D, E), all cut to size, and use the pencil and ruler to mark in the position of the grooves for the drawer bottom. Clamp both the workpiece and the guide strip (an offcut) to the bench. Push the biscuit jointer hard up against the guide strip, and run it from one side to another to cut the groove.

TIPS AND TROUBLESHOOTING

Biscuit joints Test the depth of the cut before you cut the real joints. Avoid a cut that is too shallow as this will prevent the joint from closing. You also need to ensure that the biscuit slots are not too near the edge of the boards, otherwise the saw cuts will exit the edges and ruin the appearance.

Assembling When you are clamping the frame, use protective scraps of plywood between the pine and the clamps. Do not apply excessive force; just tighten enough to close up the joint. It is important to check that the frame is perfectly square. The best way is to measure each diagonal – they should be equal. If your frame is not square, use a third sash clamp placed in line with the longest diagonal, and tighten until the diagonals are equal.

CHOPPING BOARD

This project is just about perfect. The chopping board is good to use (it is generous in size, double-sided and comfortable to handle), the form and texture are a joy to the eye (beech always looks good) and it is an exciting, skill-stretching challenge. It looks easy enough, but everything has got to be just right. If you look at the construction drawing and the step-by-step photographs, you will see that there are four basic procedures: cutting biscuit slots, routing grooves, routing tongues, and routing coves to create the handle holes. The individual procedures are straightforward, but put them together and you have quite a project. So, if you want a really smart item for your kitchen, and if you are looking to put your skills to the test, this is a good project.

YOU WILL NEED

- Compound mitre saw
- Biscuit jointer with 12 x No. 20 biscuits
- Router, 12 mm (¹⁵⁄₃₂ in) straight cutter and 6 mm (¼ in) radius cutter
- Orbital sander, 80-grit and 600-grit sandpaper
- G-clamp and 2 sash clamps
- Beech:
  A 3 pieces, 430 x 110 x 40 mm (16¹⁵⁄₁₆ x 4¹¹⁄₃₂ x 1⁹⁄₁₆ in)
  B 2 pieces, 330 x 40 x 40 mm (13 x 1⁹⁄₁₆ x 1⁹⁄₁₆ in)
- PVA glue
- Cloth for wiping up excess glue
- Clean cloth and olive oil

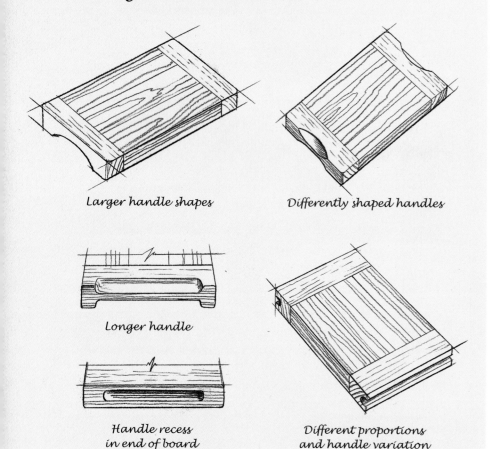

design variations

Larger handle shapes

Differently shaped handles

Longer handle

Handle recess
in end of board

Different proportions
and handle variation

Construction time: **1 weekend**
Power tools required: **biscuit jointer, router, compound mitre saw and orbital sander**

CHOPPING BOARD CONSTRUCTION DRAWING

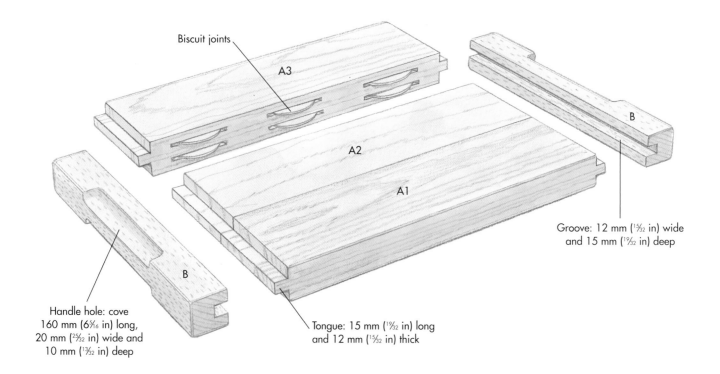

Biscuit joints

A3

A2

A1

B

Groove: 12 mm (¹⁵⁄₃₂ in) wide
and 15 mm (¹⁹⁄₃₂ in) deep

B

Handle hole: cove
160 mm (6⁵⁄₁₆ in) long,
20 mm (²⁵⁄₃₂ in) wide and
10 mm (¹³⁄₃₂ in) deep

Tongue: 15 mm (¹⁹⁄₃₂ in) long
and 12 mm (¹⁵⁄₃₂ in) thick

HOW TO BUILD THE CHOPPING BOARD

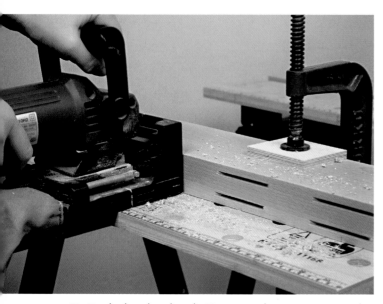

1 Cut the beech to length. Use a pencil, tape measure and square to generally establish the position of the biscuit slots, grooves, tongues and coves. Use the biscuit jointer to cut the biscuit slots in the three main boards (A1, A2, A3). Dribble PVA glue in the slots, tap the biscuits home, put the three boards together, and clamp up.

2 Take the two end strips (B), and check the marked position of the grooves. Clamp the two strips side by side on the bench, and fit the router with the straight cutter. One strip at a time, set the fence so that the cutter is centred, and then make deeper and deeper passes to cut the grooves.

3 Take the glued-up board and mark in the position of the tongues. Using the straight cutter in the router, set the fence to the length of the tongue, and make deeper and deeper passes until the rebate is complete. Repeat this procedure on both ends and both faces. Check that the end strips fit correctly; make adjustments if necessary. Spread glue on the tongues and grooves, and clamp up.

4 When the glue is dry, remove the clamps and mark the handle holes. Make a routing jig as shown or use the side fence. Clamp the workpiece to the bench, fit the router with the radius cutter, and rout the coves on both ends and both faces. Sand, then wipe with olive oil.

TIPS AND TROUBLESHOOTING

Joining the boards For best results – to achieve a board that stays flat and without gaps – it is worth checking before you start jointing that all edges are planed perfectly square to the faces of each board. Use a try square and hold the board up to the light to see if there are inaccuracies. In addition, arrange the three boards so that the growth rings (end grain) curve in alternate directions. For example: first board curved up, second board down and third board up.

Fitting the ends The tongue-and-groove joint needs to be a perfect tight fit (but not so tight that you need a mallet to close the joint) so, after cutting the grooves in the end strips, it is a good idea to practise cutting the rebates on a scrap of wood of the same thickness. It is helpful if the tongue is fractionally shorter than 15 mm (19/32 in) (14.5 mm/9/16 in for example) and then there is no doubt that the joint will close up completely on the outer faces.

CORNER SHELF CONSTRUCTION DRAWING

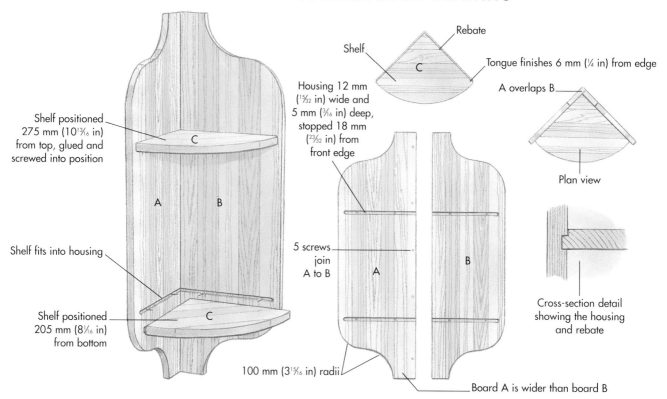

Shelf positioned 275 mm (10¹³⁄₁₆ in) from top, glued and screwed into position

Shelf fits into housing

Shelf positioned 205 mm (8⅛ in) from bottom

A

B

C

Shelf

Rebate

Housing 12 mm (¹⁵⁄₃₂ in) wide and 5 mm (³⁄₁₆ in) deep, stopped 18 mm (²³⁄₃₂ in) from front edge

Tongue finishes 6 mm (¼ in) from edge

A overlaps B

Plan view

Cross-section detail showing the housing and rebate

5 screws join A to B

A

B

100 mm (3¹⁵⁄₁₆ in) radii

Board A is wider than board B

HOW TO BUILD THE CORNER SHELF

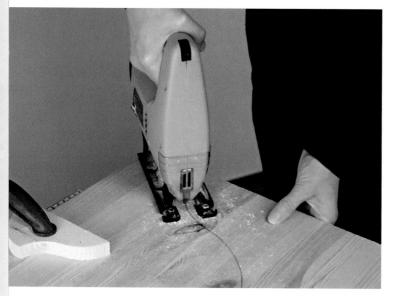

1 Use a pencil, ruler and compasses to draw the shapes on the laminated pine board – the two long boards with the smooth cyma curve ends (A, B), and the two quarter-circle shelves (C). Check that you have allowed extra wood on the back edge of one long board for the butt joint, and fret out the shapes with the jigsaw.

2 Mark in the position of the grooves and rebates – rebates on the straight edges of the shelves (C), and grooves across the two long boards (A, B). Clamp a guide strip across the workpiece, fit a straight cutter in the router, hold the router against the guide and cut the groove.

3 To rebate the straight edges of the shelves, fit the fence to the router, adjust it to match the position of the rebate, set the router against the edge, and make the cut. Try to work at a steady, easy pace, with no jerks or wobbly movements. Use a fold of fine sandpaper to rub the grooves and rebates to a smooth finish.

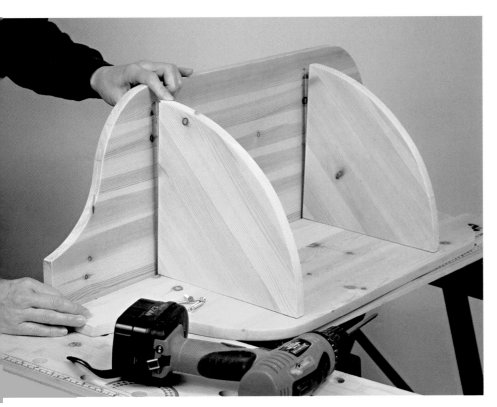

4 Have a dry-run fitting, with the rebated shelves in the housing and the two long boards (A, B) butt jointed. When you are happy with the fit, drill countersunk holes for screws through the back of A into B, and through both A and B into the shelves (C). Knock the workpiece apart, smear a small amount of glue on mating surfaces, and reassemble with screws. Finally, sand all the surfaces to a smooth finish and apply Danish oil. Re-sand and apply wax polish.

FLOWER TROUGH

When I was a child in the late 1950s, some older women in country districts were still doing their weekly wash in a wooden trough. It was reckoned that wooden vessels were much better than metal ones as they were less liable to be affected by sodas and other chemicals. A well-made trough was considered to be a valued item. Of course, when those newfangled washing machines took over – my granny called them 'swish-swash-mangle-tangles' – the poor old trough was demoted and used, more often than not, for displaying plants. The design is quite sophisticated: not only are the end boards set into grooves in the side boards, but all four sides are canted out at an angle.

YOU WILL NEED

- Jigsaw

- Compound mitre saw

- Orbital sander and 80-grit sandpaper

- Cordless driver, counter-bore drill bit and screwdriver bit to match screws

- Router and 12 mm ($^{15}/_{32}$ in) straight cutter

- G-clamp and quick-release clamp

- Smoothing plane

- Pine tongue-and-groove boards to make up the following areas:
  A 2 pieces, 680 x 270 x 18 mm (26$^{25}/_{32}$ x 10$^{5}/_{8}$ x $^{23}/_{32}$ in)
  B 2 pieces, 450 x 330 x 18 mm (17$^{23}/_{32}$ x 13 x $^{23}/_{32}$ in)

- Pine:
  C 2 pieces, 550 x 145 x 18 mm (21$^{21}/_{32}$ x 5$^{23}/_{32}$ x $^{23}/_{32}$ in)
  D 4 pieces, 288 x 70 x 18 mm (11$^{11}/_{32}$ x 2$^{3}/_{4}$ x $^{23}/_{32}$ in)
  E 2 pieces, 253 x 70 x 18 mm (9$^{31}/_{32}$ x 2$^{3}/_{4}$ x $^{23}/_{32}$ in)
  F 2 pieces, 268 x 70 x 18 mm (10$^{9}/_{16}$ x 2$^{3}/_{4}$ x $^{23}/_{32}$ in)

- No. 8 crossheaded screws: 46 x 30 mm (1$^{3}/_{16}$ in) long

- Dowel and 80-grit sandpaper

- Filler

- Paintbrush

- Paint of your choice

design variations

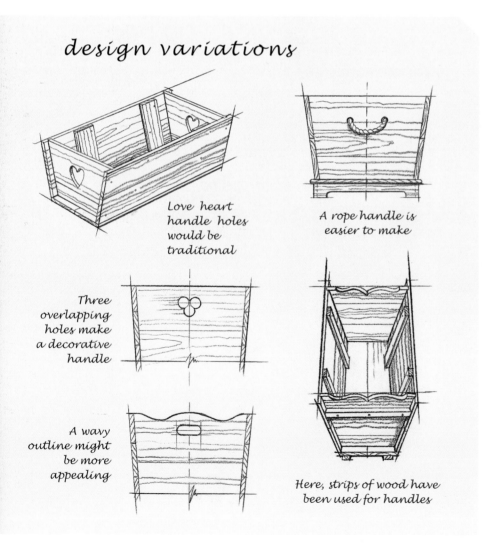

Love heart handle holes would be traditional

A rope handle is easier to make

Three overlapping holes make a decorative handle

A wavy outline might be more appealing

Here, strips of wood have been used for handles

Construction time: 1 weekend

Power tools required: compound mitre saw, jigsaw, cordless driver, router and orbital sander

FLOWER TROUGH CONSTRUCTION DRAWING

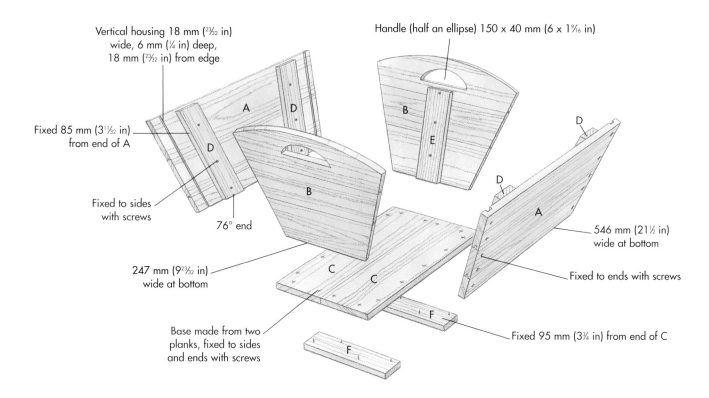

Vertical housing 18 mm (²³⁄₃₂ in) wide, 6 mm (¼ in) deep, 18 mm (²³⁄₃₂ in) from edge

Handle (half an ellipse) 150 x 40 mm (6 x 1⁹⁄₁₆ in)

Fixed 85 mm (3¹¹⁄₃₂ in) from end of A

Fixed to sides with screws

76° end

247 mm (9²³⁄₃₂ in) wide at bottom

Base made from two planks, fixed to sides and ends with screws

546 mm (21½ in) wide at bottom

Fixed to ends with screws

Fixed 95 mm (3¾ in) from end of C

HOW TO BUILD THE FLOWER TROUGH

1 Mark out the sides and ends (A, B) on the loosely assembled (not screwed) tongue-and-groove boards. Cut them out with the jigsaw. Cut out the battens (D, E, F) with the compound mitre saw. Assemble the ends (B, E), mark out the handle holes and cut them out with the jigsaw. Use a dowel and sandpaper to sand the edges to a rounded finish.

2 Assemble the sides (A) and battens (D) using 3 screws for each batten. Make sure each of the tongue-and-groove boards is attached to the batten. The battens run parallel (at the same angle) to the housings, and are used as guides for routing against. Check the size of your router's base plate and modify the position of the battens if necessary.

3 Clamp the side boards (A) securely to the bench, have another check to make sure that the batten guides are correctly placed in relation to the size of the router, then use the router to cut the grooves.

4 Have a trial fitting of the four sides, note the angle at which the end boards meet the grooves, and use the hand plane to modify the end boards accordingly. (This stage is tricky, and you might need help.) Set the end boards in the grooves and fix them with screws.

5 Clamp the box on the bench so that the bottom edge is uppermost, and use the hand plane to skim the bottom edges to a level finish. Finally, screw the base (C and F) in place, and fill the counter-bored holes to conceal the screws. Give all sawn edges a rub down, and give the trough a coat of paint in the colour of your choice.

TIPS AND TROUBLESHOOTING

Tongue-and-groove boards These give the trough a rustic appearance but they are quite difficult to assemble. To make the project easier, use pine block board (the sides and ends can be cut from single sheets) and you no longer need battens D and E. With no battens to rout against to produce the housings, you would have to use the router fence. If using block board, you may need to use more screws to join the sides to the ends.

Housings If you do not have a router or prefer not to cut the housings, use strips of wood and screws at each corner to join the sides to the ends.

Screws For a longer-lasting, antique appearance, use either copper nails or countersunk brass slot-headed screws in place of the recessed crossheaded screws.

BAR STOOL

This is the perfect stool for a super-modern, design-conscious kitchen. No more creaky old crumbling bits of plastic and plywood left over from the worst glitz-and-glitter designs of the last century – especially the 1970s and 1980s, which produced some very tasteless pieces of furniture – now you can have a modern classic that belongs in the 21st century. Drawing inspiration from those chunky pieces of Mission furniture from the 1920s and 1930s, and made from a mix of good-quality pine, pine block board and stainless-steel tubing, this is one of the easiest projects in the book.

YOU WILL NEED

- Jigsaw

- Compound mitre saw

- Drill press and 25 mm ($^{31}/_{32}$ in) forstner bit

- Cordless driver, 3 mm ($^{1}/_{8}$ in) twist bit (not brad point), countersink bit and screwdriver bit to fit your screws

- Router, 12 mm ($^{15}/_{32}$ in) straight cutter and 6 mm ($^{1}/_{4}$ in) round-over cutter

- Orbital sander, 80-grit and 600-grit sandpaper

- G-clamp and 2 sash clamps

- Smoothing plane

- Bevel-edged chisel

- Tenon saw

- Pine block board:
  A 1 piece, 325 x 325 x 18 mm ($12^{25}/_{32}$ x $12^{25}/_{32}$ x $^{23}/_{32}$ in)

- Pine:
  B 4 pieces, 260 x 87 x 37 mm ($10^{7}/_{32}$ x $3^{7}/_{16}$ x $1^{15}/_{32}$ in)
  C 4 pieces, 630 x 42 x 42 mm ($24^{13}/_{16}$ x $1^{21}/_{32}$ x $1^{21}/_{32}$ in)

- Stainless-steel tubing:
  D 6 pieces, 251 mm ($9^{7}/_{8}$ in) long and 25 mm ($^{31}/_{32}$ in) in diameter

- 4 expansion plates, 25 x 25 x 25 mm ($^{31}/_{32}$ x $^{31}/_{32}$ x $^{31}/_{32}$ in)

- 20 x No. 8 screws, 15 mm ($^{19}/_{32}$ in) long

- PVA glue

- Finishing oil

- Cloths for wiping up excess glue and applying oil

design variations

An alternative seat shape and handle idea

Rationalize the design and make it as simple as possible

A shorter stool with bevel-edged details

A stool or hall table with a small drawer

A round seat and arched rails

Construction time: 2 weekends

Power tools required: compound mitre saw, jigsaw, router, cordless driver, drill press and orbital sander

BAR STOOL CONSTRUCTION DRAWING

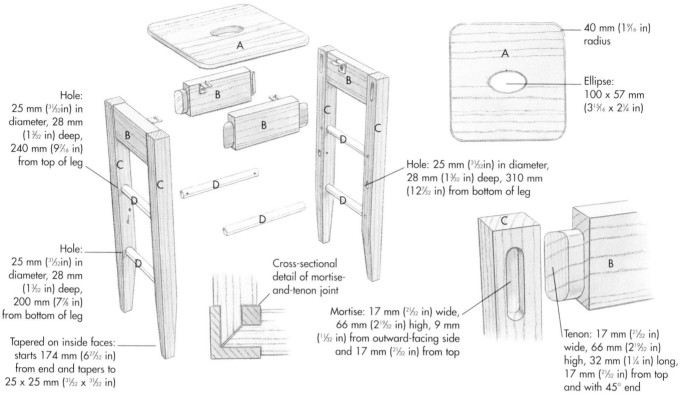

40 mm (1⁹⁄₁₆ in) radius

Ellipse: 100 x 57 mm (3¹⁵⁄₁₆ x 2¼ in)

Hole: 25 mm (³¹⁄₃₂in) in diameter, 28 mm (1³⁄₃₂ in) deep, 240 mm (9⁷⁄₁₆ in) from top of leg

Hole: 25 mm (³¹⁄₃₂in) in diameter, 28 mm (1³⁄₃₂ in) deep, 200 mm (7⅞ in) from bottom of leg

Tapered on inside faces: starts 174 mm (6²⁷⁄₃₂ in) from end and tapers to 25 x 25 mm (³¹⁄₃₂ x ³¹⁄₃₂ in)

Hole: 25 mm (³¹⁄₃₂in) in diameter, 28 mm (1³⁄₃₂ in) deep, 310 mm (12⁷⁄₃₂ in) from bottom of leg

Cross-sectional detail of mortise-and-tenon joint

Mortise: 17 mm (²¹⁄₃₂ in) wide, 66 mm (2¹⁹⁄₃₂ in) high, 9 mm (¹¹⁄₃₂ in) from outward-facing side and 17 mm (²¹⁄₃₂ in) from top

Tenon: 17 mm (²¹⁄₃₂ in) wide, 66 mm (2¹⁹⁄₃₂ in) high, 32 mm (1¼ in) long, 17 mm (²¹⁄₃₂ in) from top and with 45° end

HOW TO BUILD THE BAR STOOL

1 Use the compound mitre saw to cut the legs (C) and the apron pieces (B) to length, and the jigsaw to cut out the seat slab (A). Draw the handle hole at the centre of the seat using an ellipse. Drill a pilot hole in the waste, enter the blade of the jigsaw and fret out the hole. Use a round-over router cutter to give the edges of the seat a rounded profile.

2 Build a jig for routing the tenons, using pine of the same section as the aprons (B) and a piece of scrap plywood. Enter an apron piece (B) in the jig. Using the straight cutter in the router, establish the shoulder. Withdraw the workpiece slightly then continue routing to clear the waste. Use the tenon saw and the bevel-edged chisel to finish shaping the tenons.

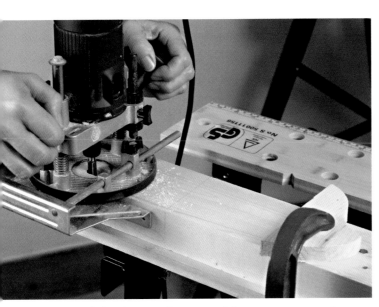

3 Mark the shape and position of the mortises: two at the top end of each leg (C). One piece at a time, clamp a leg to the workbench and use the router to cut the mortises. Work repeatedly deeper and deeper cuts until the two mortises meet within the body of the top of the leg.

4 Use a pencil, ruler and square to mark the taper on the bottom of the legs. Cut away the waste with the jigsaw, and use the plane and the sander to smooth the surfaces. Study the drawings to establish the position of the stainless-steel stretchers on the legs (D), and pencil in centre points as a guide for the drill.

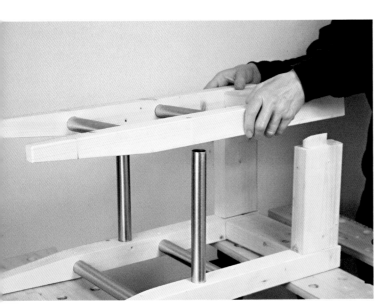

5 Use the drill press and forstner bit to sink the holes. Glue and clamp the joints so that the frame of the stool is square and the tubes contained. (Drill 3 mm/⅛ in holes into the legs and through one side of the metal tube at a slight angle in order to give you room to manoeuvre the drill.) Fix the tube ends with screws.

6 When the glue is dry, remove the clamps and use a scrap of sandpaper to tidy up. Screw the expansion plates first to the inside of the frame and then to the seat slab. Make sure you have the slots arranged so as to allow the wood to move across the run of the grain. Finish with two applications of oil.

WINDOW BOX

This project looks to the domestic woodwork that was produced in England and America in the first quarter of the 20th century – the sort of basic woodwork that was made by our ancestors. With a project like a window box, the whole focus of the exercise would have been how to make a good, strong item with the minimum of effort and expense. Such woodwork was characterized by being ornate, yet very simple in construction – to the extent that it could be built with basic hand tools and spiked together with nails. Our project updates this traditional approach by using a low-cost compound mitre saw.

YOU WILL NEED

- Compound mitre saw

- Cordless driver, screwdriver bit to fit your screws and counter-bore bit

- Orbital sander and 80-grit sandpaper

- Crossheaded screwdriver

- Pine:
  A 4 pieces, 794 x 32 x 32 mm (31¼ x 1¼ x 1¼ in)
  B 4 pieces, 218 x 32 x 32 mm (8¹⁹⁄₃₂ x 1¼ x 1¼ in)
  C 4 pieces, 250 x 45 x 45 mm (9²⁷⁄₃₂ x 1²⁵⁄₃₂ x 1²⁵⁄₃₂ in)
  D 26 pieces, 250 x 70 x 18 mm (9²⁷⁄₃₂ x 2¾ x ²³⁄₃₂ in)
  E 10 pieces, 218 x 70 x 18 mm (8¹⁹⁄₃₂ x 2¾ x ²³⁄₃₂ in)

- Crossheaded screws: 68 x No. 8, 40 mm (1⁹⁄₁₆ in) long

- Wood-coloured filler

- Matt white paint

- Paintbrush

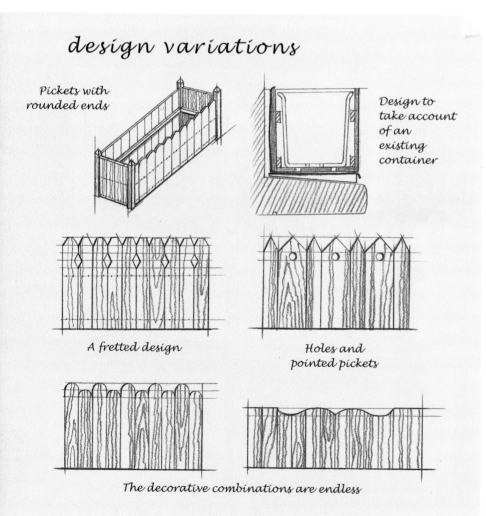

design variations

Pickets with rounded ends

Design to take account of an existing container

A fretted design

Holes and pointed pickets

The decorative combinations are endless

Construction time: **1 weekend**

Power tools required: **compound mitre saw, cordless driver and orbital sander**

WINDOW BOX CONSTRUCTION DRAWING

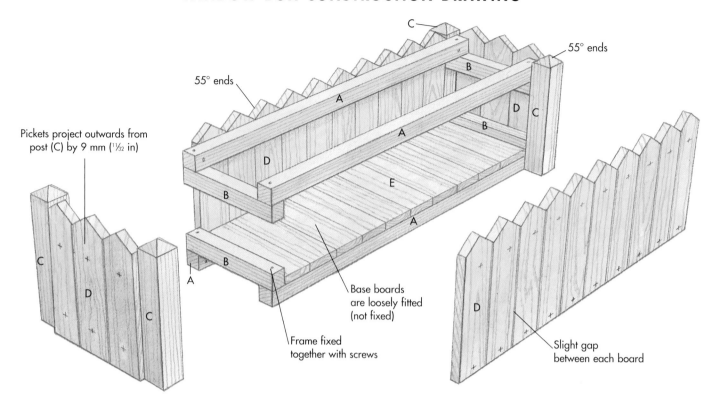

C

55° ends

55° ends

B

A

D C

B

A

Pickets project outwards from post (C) by 9 mm ($^{11}/_{32}$ in)

D

C

D

C

B

A

D

E

A

A

B

Base boards are loosely fitted (not fixed)

Frame fixed together with screws

D

Slight gap between each board

HOW TO BUILD THE WINDOW BOX

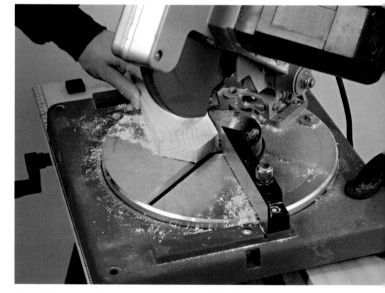

1 Cut the components to length – 4 of (A) and 4 of (B) for the frame, 4 corner posts (C), 26 pickets (D) and 10 base boards (E). Set the mitre saw to an angle of 55°. Take the corner posts and use a pencil, ruler and square to mark one end as the top. One face at a time, saw down through the centre line of the top end to achieve a pyramidal shape.

2 Take the pickets (D) and use a pencil, ruler and square to mark a centre line and a shoulder line on one end. Keep the mitre saw set to an angle of 55°. One picket at a time, saw down through the centre line – first one side and then the other – to achieve the characteristic picket shape.

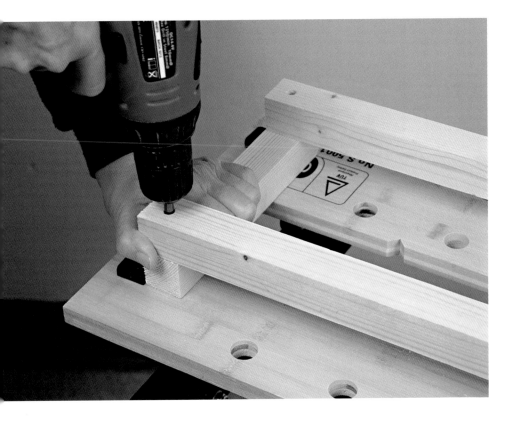

3 Set the frame pieces (A, B) together to make two identical rectangular frames. Drill counter-bored holes halfway down through the top member of the corner butt joint. One corner at a time, drive one screw down through the butted joint, check for squareness and then clench the screws tightly.

4 Set the two rectangular frames together so that they are mirror-imaged with the short rails looking towards each other, and so that they are flush with the inner faces of the corner posts. Drill counter-bored holes (at an angle that allows access for the drill) and screw the frames to the corner posts. You might need to use a hand screwdriver.

5 Screw the pickets to the frame and set the base boards (E) in place (these are not fixed). Finally, rub down the surfaces to remove whiskers of wood, and give the whole box a wash of matt white paint.

CHILD'S WORKTABLE

This design draws its inspiration from the furniture of the early 1950s. Such pieces have certain things in common: they have a characteristic round-cornered shape (like variations on the shape of an artist's painting palette), the surfaces are either left plain or are brightly coloured with gloss enamel paints, the construction is direct and uncomplicated, and, most importantly of all, they are made from thick sheets of plywood, with the fixings and the edges of the plywood on view. If you like working with plywood and want to make a 1950s retro piece, and know of a child who is just the right age for a worktable, this is a good project.

design variations

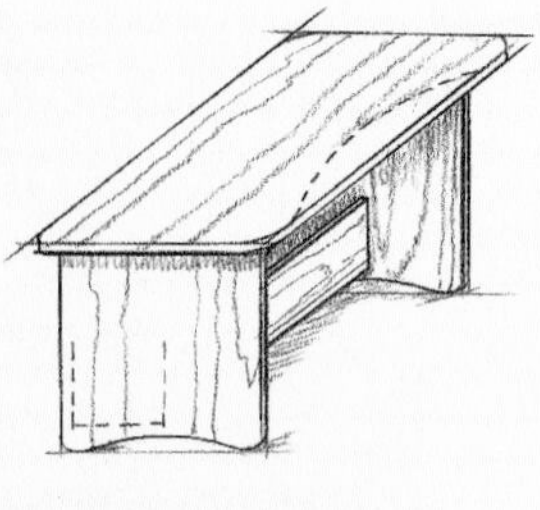

A simple design that could be modified

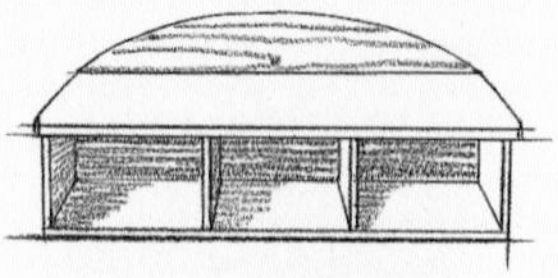

A wall-mounted unit for working at and storing pens and paints

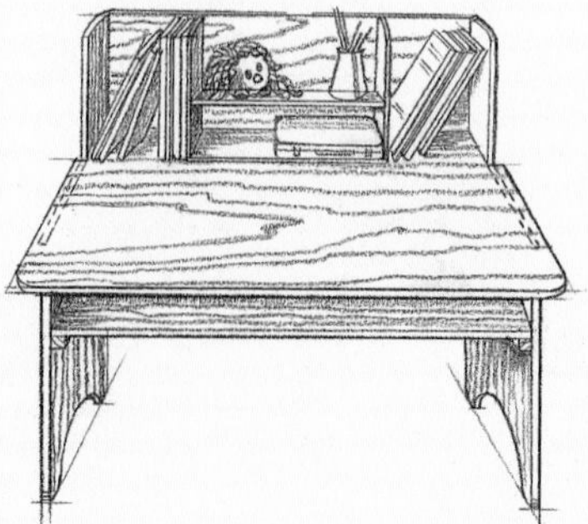

A traditional rectangular shape may be more to your taste

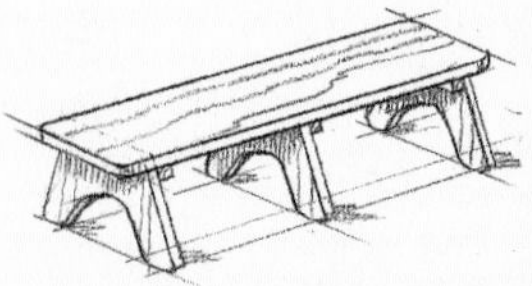

A low table for working at while sitting on the floor

YOU WILL NEED

- Compasses
- Jigsaw
- Compound mitre saw
- Drill and 12 mm (15/32 in) twist bit with a brad point
- Cordless driver, screwdriver bit to fit your screws and counter-bore bit
- Router and 4 mm (5/32 in) straight cutter
- Orbital sander, 80-grit and 600-grit sandpaper
- Palm sander
- 2 G-clamps
- Crosshead screwdriver
- Pin hammer
- Block plane
- Tenon saw
- Birch plywood:
  A 1 piece, 600 x 600 x 13 mm (23 5/8 x 23 5/8 x 1/2 in)
  B 4 pieces, 527 x 444 x 13 mm (20 3/4 x 17 15/32 x 1/2 in)
  E 2 pieces, 383 x 143.5 x 9.5 mm (15 3/32 x 5 21/32 x 3/8 in)
  F 2 pieces, 143.5 x 120 x 9.5 mm (5 21/32 x 4 23/32 x 3/8 in)
  G 1 piece, 372 x 128 x 4.5 mm (14 21/32 x 5 1/32 x 3/16 in)
  H 12 pieces, 120 x 120 x 9.5 mm (4 23/32 x 4 23/32 x 3/8 in)
  I 3 pieces, 109 x 128 x 4.5 mm (5 3/16 x 4 9/32 x 3/16 in)
  K 4 pieces, 78 x 64 x 9.5 mm (3 1/16 x 2 17/32 x 3/8 in)
  L 1 piece, 54.5 x 54.5 x 9.5 mm (2 5/32 x 2 5/32 x 3/8 in)
  M 1 piece, 300 x 78 x 9.5 mm (11 13/16 x 3 1/16 x 3/8 in)
  N 1 piece, 66 x 58 x 9.5 mm (2 19/32 x 2 1/4 x 3/8 in)
- Pine:
  C 4 pieces, 261 x 35 x 35 mm (10 9/32 x 1 3/8 x 1 3/8 in)
  D 1 piece, 170 x 35 x 35 mm (6 11/16 x 1 3/8 x 1 3/8 in)
  J 1 piece, 78 x 72 x 72 mm (3 1/16 x 2 27/32 x 2 27/32 in)
  O 1 piece, 32 x 32 x 32 mm (1 1/4 x 1 1/4 x 1 1/4 in)
  P 1 piece, 32 x 32 x 32 mm (1 1/4 x 1 1/4 x 1 1/4 in)
  Q 1 piece, 43 x 37 x 32 mm (1 11/16 x 1 15/32 x 1 1/4 in)
- Veneer pins
- Crossheaded screws: 20 x No. 8, 40 mm (1 9/16 in) long
- Wood-coloured filler
- PVA glue
- Finishing oil
- Cloths for wiping up excess glue and applying oil

Construction time: 2 weekends

Power tools required: jigsaw, orbital sander, cordless driver, drill, compound mitre saw, router and palm sander

CHILD'S WORKTABLE CONSTRUCTION DRAWING

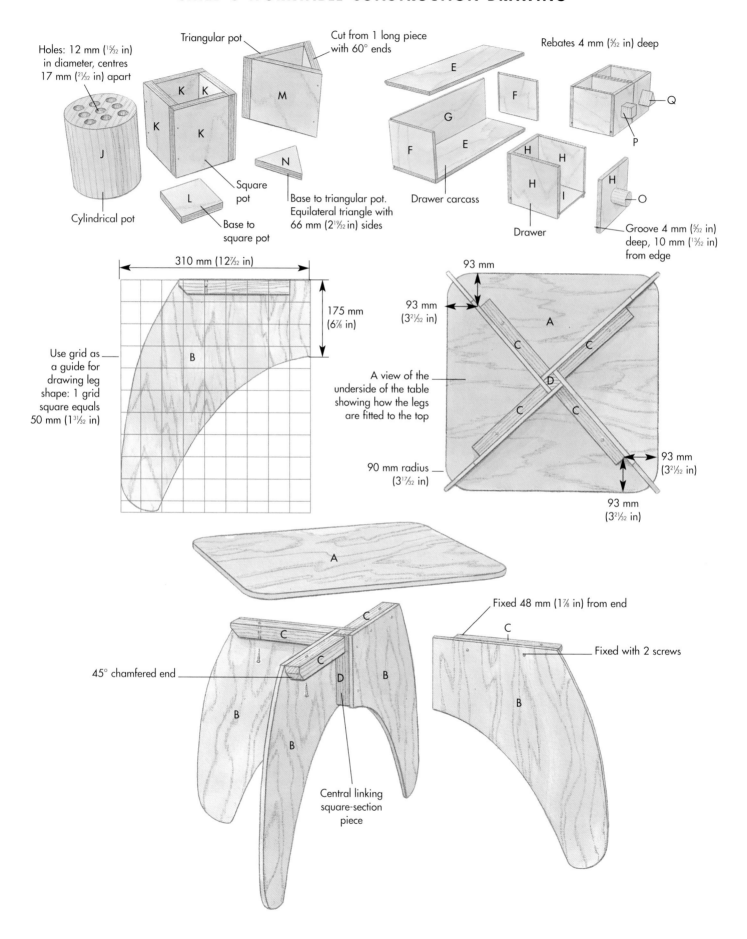

Holes: 12 mm (¹⁵⁄₃₂ in) in diameter, centres 17 mm (²¹⁄₃₂ in) apart

Triangular pot

Cut from 1 long piece with 60° ends

Rebates 4 mm (⁵⁄₃₂ in) deep

E

F

G

F

E

Q

P

H

H

H

H

I

H

O

Drawer carcass

Drawer

Groove 4 mm (⁵⁄₃₂ in) deep, 10 mm (¹³⁄₃₂ in) from edge

Cylindrical pot

J

K K
K K

Square pot

L

Base to square pot

N

Base to triangular pot. Equilateral triangle with 66 mm (2¹⁹⁄₃₂ in) sides

M

310 mm (12⁷⁄₃₂ in)

175 mm (6⁷⁄₈ in)

Use grid as a guide for drawing leg shape: 1 grid square equals 50 mm (1³¹⁄₃₂ in)

B

93 mm

93 mm (3²¹⁄₃₂ in)

A

C   C

C   C

D

A view of the underside of the table showing how the legs are fitted to the top

93 mm (3²¹⁄₃₂ in)

90 mm radius (3¹⁷⁄₃₂ in)

93 mm (3²¹⁄₃₂ in)

A

Fixed 48 mm (1⁷⁄₈ in) from end

C

45° chamfered end

C
C

D

B

Fixed with 2 screws

B

B

B

Central linking square-section piece

HOW TO BUILD THE CHILD'S WORKTABLE

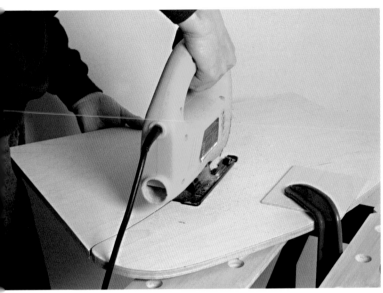

1 Mark out the shapes of the components on the two thicknesses of birch plywood – the table top (A), four legs (B) (using the grid as a guide), and the various pieces that make the drawers (E, F, G, H, I) and table pots (K, L, M, N). Double-check that the measurements are correct, then cut out the various parts with the jigsaw.

2 Make sure, when you are cutting the four legs (B), that you finish up with four identical profiles. Pay particular attention to the 90° angle at the top of each leg, and the total top-to-floor drop height.

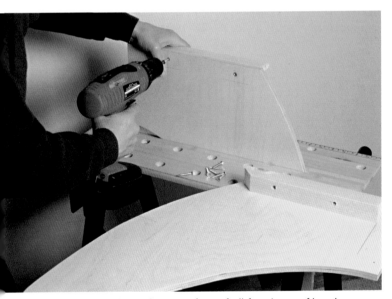

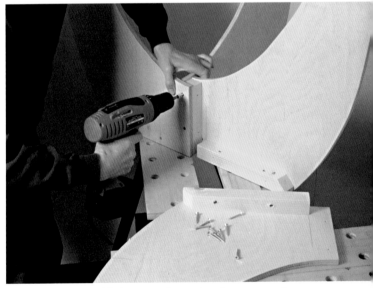

3 Mark, on the same face of all four leg profiles, the position of the leg-to-top square section (C), and the central linking square section (D). Cut the five lengths of pine to size, and carefully screw the four long lengths (C) in place – one length to the top edge of each of the four leg profiles.

4 Take the central linking member (D) and screw it to the face of one of the leg profiles (B). When you are happy with the placing, work around the central linking member screwing the other three legs in place. Stand the four-legged unit upright and make adjustments until the top edges are level, one to another.

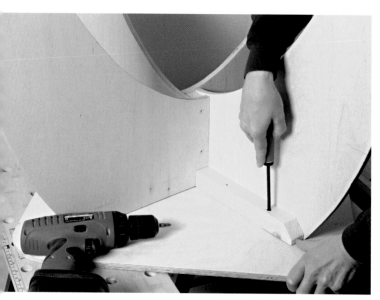

5 Set the table top on a smooth surface with the best face downwards. Flip the four-legged unit over so that it is upside down, and centre it on the table top. Draw in guide marks, drill necessary pilot holes and fix with screws.

6 Take the four pieces of plywood that go to make the sides of the drawer carcass – base board (E), top board (E) and two end boards (F) – and use the router to run a rebate on what will be the inside back edge of the box. Glue and pin the top and sides together, then glue and pin the back board (G) in place in the rebate.

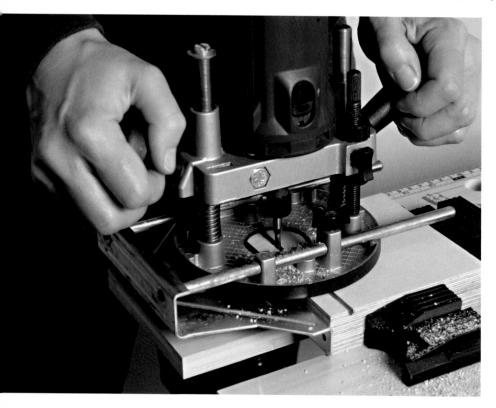

7 Take the 15 pieces that go to make the three drawers (H, I), and label them so that you can see what goes where. One piece at a time, take the front, back and side boards (H), and pencil in the position of the groove. Set the fence on the router and cut the grooves. Glue and pin the drawers together. Make the three knobs (O, P, Q) from three offcuts of pine. Use the tenon saw and block plane to cut and shape them.

8 Cut 60° ends on the sides of the pieces of plywood for the triangular pot (M). Join the sides (M) and base (N) together using pins and glue. Sand smooth with the palm sander. Assemble the square pot (K, L) in the same way.

9 When you come to making the cylindrical pot (J), use the compass to draw the circle on both ends of the wood, drill out the pattern of nine holes, and use the block plane and sandpaper to create the circular shape. Finally, give all surfaces of the worktable two coats of oil.

TIPS AND TROUBLESHOOTING

Choosing plywood Don't think that you can cut costs by using a cheaper grade of plywood. Yes, the top-grade birch plywood is expensive, but against that, the layers are so well glued and packed that the edges are always free from cavities.

Cutting the plywood with the jigsaw Fit a new fine-toothed blade at the start of the project. Work at a steady pace, all the while being ready to turn the wood and manoeuvre the saw so that the blade is presented with the line of the next cut.

Making the cylindrical pot Make sure, when you are choosing the wood, that you go for a piece that is straight-grained and free from splits and knots.

COMPUTER WORKSTATION

One day, I was sitting in my office-studio, just looking and dreaming, and it suddenly came to me that the whole place was a mess. The computer was sitting on the floor, the monitor was propped up on a pile of books, the whole table was littered with paper, but worst of all, there were wires and cables crawling all over the place. I decided, then and there, that what I needed was a made-to-measure computer workstation. If you look at the construction drawings, you will see that the joy of this project is not so much in its aesthetic good looks, but rather in its functional flexibility. You can shape the arrangement of shelves, boxes, trays and holes to suit your own needs.

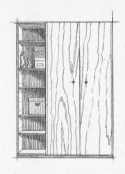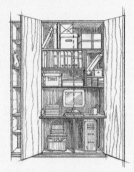

design variations

A large wall unit for storing all your office equipment. A vertical tambour door (see page 96) may work for this design

YOU WILL NEED

- Jigsaw

- Drill, twist bits and forstner bit to suit cam dowels, and hole saw

- Cordless driver, screwdriver bit to fit your screws and counter-bore bit

- Router, 4 mm (⁵⁄₃₂ in) and 12 mm (¹⁵⁄₃₂ in) straight cutters

- Orbital sander, 80-grit and 600-grit sandpaper

- 2 G-clamps

- Birch plywood:
  A 2 pieces, 1216 x 535 x 25.5 mm (47⅞ x 21¹⁄₁₆ x 1 in)
  B 2 pieces, 890 x 560 x 25.5 mm (35¹⁄₃₂ x 22¹⁄₁₆ x 1 in)
  C 1 piece, 799 x 520.5 x 25.5 mm (31¹⁵⁄₃₂ x 20½ x 1 in)
  D 1 piece, 799 x 520.5 x 17 mm (31¹⁵⁄₃₂ x 20½ x 2¹⁄₃₂ in)
  E 1 piece, 630 x 520.5 x 17 mm (24¹³⁄₁₆ x 20½ x 2¹⁄₃₂ in)
  F 1 piece, 680 x 520.5 x 17 mm (26²⁵⁄₃₂ x 20½ x 2¹⁄₃₂ in)
  G 1 piece, 557 x 520.5 x 17 mm (21²⁹⁄₃₂ x 20½ x 2¹⁄₃₂ in)
  H 1 piece, 520.5 x 152 x 17 mm (20½ x 6 x 2¹⁄₃₂ in)
  I 1 piece, 520.5 x 162 x 17 mm (20½ x 6⅜ x 2¹⁄₃₂ in)

J 2 pieces, 1202 x 414 x 17 mm (47⁵⁄₁₆ x 16⁵⁄₁₆ x 2¹⁄₃₂ in)
K 1 piece, 1236 x 819 x 4.5 mm (48²¹⁄₃₂ x 32¼ x ³⁄₁₆ in)
L 6 pieces, 501.5 x 160 x 9.5 mm (19¾ x 6⁵⁄₁₆ x ⅜ in)
M 6 pieces, 160 x 151 x 9.5 mm (6⁵⁄₁₆ x 5¹⁵⁄₁₆ x ⅜ in)
N 3 pieces, 140.5 x 132 x 9.5 mm (5¹⁷⁄₃₂ x 5³⁄₁₆ x ⅜ in)
O 3 pieces, 509.5 x 140 x 4.5 mm (20¹⁄₁₆ x 5½ x ³⁄₁₆ in)

- Maple:
  A1 2 pieces, 1216 x 25.5 x 5 mm (47⅞ x 1 x ³⁄₁₆ in)
  B1 2 pieces, 900 x 25.5 x 5 mm (35⁷⁄₁₆ x 1 x ³⁄₁₆ in)
  B2 4 pieces, 560 x 25.5 x 5 mm (22¹⁄₁₆ x 1 x ³⁄₁₆ in)
  C1 1 piece, 799 x 25.5 x 5 mm (31¹⁵⁄₃₂ x 1 x ³⁄₁₆ in)
  D1 1 piece, 799 x 17 x 5 mm (31¹⁵⁄₃₂ x 2¹⁄₃₂ x ³⁄₁₆ in)
  E1 1 piece, 630 x 17 x 5 mm (24¹³⁄₁₆ x 2¹⁄₃₂ x ³⁄₁₆ in)
  F1 1 piece, 690 x 17 x 5 mm (27⁵⁄₃₂ x 2¹⁄₃₂ x ³⁄₁₆ in)
  F2 2 pieces, 520.5 x 17 x 5 mm (20½ x 2¹⁄₃₂ x ³⁄₁₆ in)
  G1 1 piece, 557 x 17 x 5 mm (21²⁹⁄₃₂ x 2¹⁄₃₂ x ³⁄₁₆ in)
  H1 1 piece, 152 x 17 x 5 mm (6 x 2¹⁄₃₂ x ³⁄₁₆ in)

I1 1 piece, 162 x 17 x 5 mm (6⅜ x 2¹⁄₃₂ x ³⁄₁₆ in)
J1 4 pieces, 1202 x 17 x 5 mm (47⁵⁄₁₆ x 2¹⁄₃₂ x ³⁄₁₆ in)
J2 4 pieces, 424 x 17 x 5 mm (16¹¹⁄₁₆ x 2¹⁄₃₂ x ³⁄₁₆ in)

- Pin hammer

- 32 cam dowel fixings

- 10 x 25 mm (³¹⁄₃₂ in) No. 6 screws

- 6 x 20 mm (²⁵⁄₃₂ in) hinges with screws

- 2 magnetic catches with screws

- 2 drawer runners with 15 mm (¹⁹⁄₃₂ in) screws

- Veneer pins

- 4 swivelling castors with wheels 70 mm (2¾ in) in diameter and 20 mm (²⁵⁄₃₂ in) screws to fix

- Wood-coloured filler

- PVA glue

- Danish oil

- Cloths for wiping up excess glue and applying oil

Construction time: **3 weekends**

Power tools required: **jigsaw, drill, router, cordless driver and orbital sander**

COMPUTER WORKSTATION CONSTRUCTION DRAWING

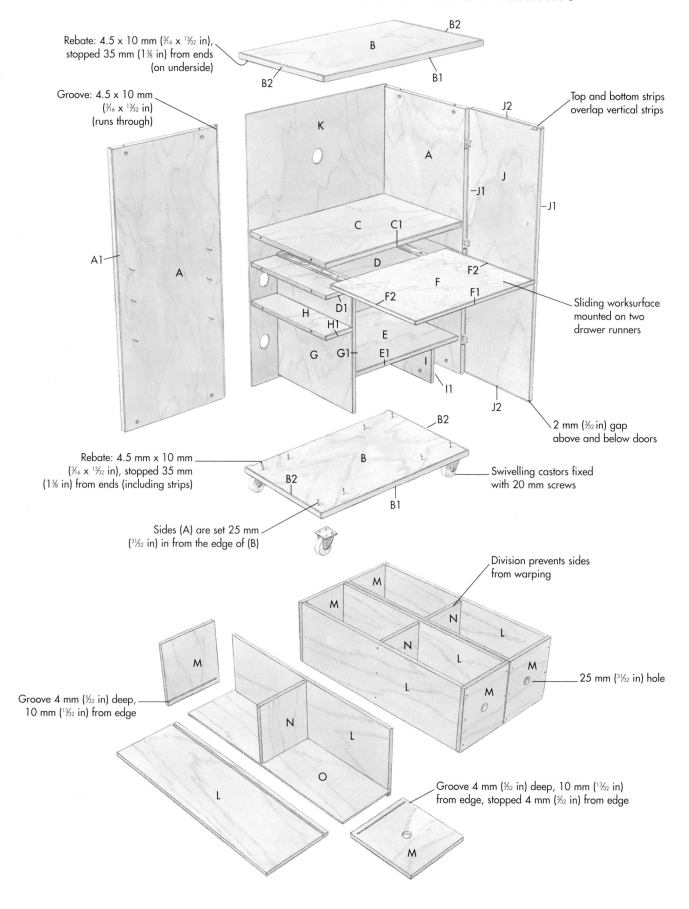

Rebate: 4.5 x 10 mm (³⁄₁₆ x ¹³⁄₃₂ in), stopped 35 mm (1³⁄₈ in) from ends (on underside)

Groove: 4.5 x 10 mm (³⁄₁₆ x ¹³⁄₃₂ in) (runs through)

Top and bottom strips overlap vertical strips

Sliding worksurface mounted on two drawer runners

2 mm (³⁄₃₂ in) gap above and below doors

Rebate: 4.5 mm x 10 mm (³⁄₁₆ x ¹³⁄₃₂ in), stopped 35 mm (1³⁄₈ in) from ends (including strips)

Swivelling castors fixed with 20 mm screws

Sides (A) are set 25 mm (³¹⁄₃₂ in) in from the edge of (B)

Division prevents sides from warping

25 mm (³¹⁄₃₂ in) hole

Groove 4 mm (⁵⁄₃₂ in) deep, 10 mm (¹³⁄₃₂ in) from edge

Groove 4 mm (⁵⁄₃₂ in) deep, 10 mm (¹³⁄₃₂ in) from edge, stopped 4 mm (⁵⁄₃₂ in) from edge

B, B1, B2, K, A, A1, J2, J, J1, C, C1, D, F, F1, F2, D1, H, H1, E, E1, G, G1, I, I1, M, N, L, O

HOW TO BUILD THE COMPUTER WORKSTATION

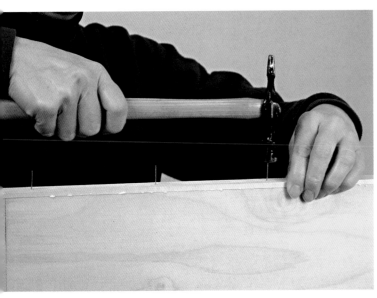

1 Use a pencil, tape measure and square to establish the size of the various pieces of plywood. Cut them out with the jigsaw. Glue and pin the strips of maple on the edges of the doors, sides, top and bottom pieces, and shelves. Knock the pinheads below the surface of the wood and fill the holes with wood-coloured filler.

2 Use the hole saw to cut 65 mm (2⁹⁄₁₆ in) holes in the back of the unit (K) for computer cables to pass through – the holes should occur in the centre of each compartment once assembled. Identify the positions of the rebates in the top, bottom and sides (A, B), then use the router and 12 mm (¹⁵⁄₃₂ in) cutter to cut them accordingly.

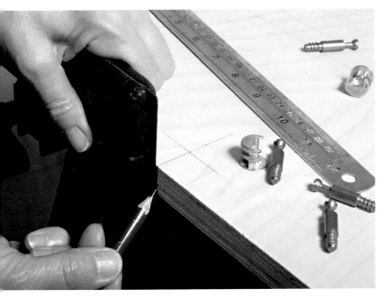

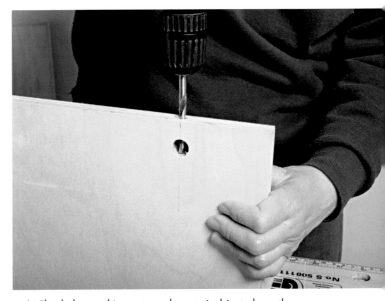

3 Once you have prepared all the plywood sheets that go to make up the design, all variously edged, drilled and rubbed down to a smooth-edged finish, use a pencil, tape measure and square to carefully mark in the position of the metal cam dowels – the cam holes on the face of the ply, and the dowel holes on edges and faces.

4 Check the marking out, and use twist bits to bore the holes for the cam dowels. Drill shallow pilot holes in the face of the ply for the screw end, and deep holes in the edge for the shaft. Use the forstner bit to bore the large cam holes. Make sure that the shaft and cam holes are aligned and centred one to another.

5 Use the pencil and tape measure to mark in, on the underside of the keyboard surface (F) and the undershelf support (D), the precise position of the metal runners. Screw the metal tracks and roller strips in place. Check the action and make necessary adjustments.

6 Assemble the central boards (D, E, G, H, I); locate the dowels, insert the cams and tighten them with a screwdriver. Fit one side piece (A), the undershelf support (D) with the keyboard surface (F) attached, and the top shelf (C), tightening the fixings as you progress. The second side (A) can then be fitted, followed by the top and the base (B).

7 Once you have achieved the basic carcass, take the back board (K) (all drilled and rubbed down), and have a trial fitting in the rebate at the back of the unit. Ease and adjust as necessary, and screw it in place.

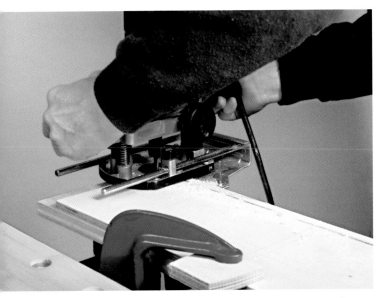

8 Take the pieces that go to make the CD drawers – the back, front and sides (L, M) – and mark in the position of the stopped and through grooves. Fit the router with the 4 mm (⁵⁄₃₂ in) cutter, set the fence and cut the grooves accordingly. Drill 25 mm (³¹⁄₃₂ in) holes through the front pieces using the hole saw.

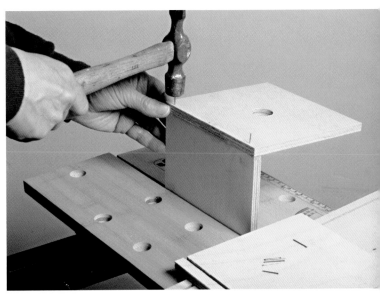

9 Assemble the drawers using glue and pins (the base of each drawer fits in the grooves and is not glued). The divisions (N) are fitted last. Fit the swivelling castors to the base using 20 mm (²⁵⁄₃₂ in) screws.

10 Mark out the position of the hinges on the doors and sides. Take the doors and screw the hinges in place. Align the doors with the carcass (support the door on a pile of offcuts) and attach the other flap of the hinge. Rub all the surfaces to a smooth finish. Finally, give the surfaces a couple of coats of Danish oil.

TIPS AND TROUBLESHOOTING

Edging the plywood Though we have chosen to trim the on-view edges of plywood with strips of maple, there is no reason why you can't sand the edges of plywood to a good, smooth finish and have them as a design feature.

Cam dowel fixings There is no denying that the cam dowel fixings are both expensive and somewhat tricky to fit. If you want to cut costs and go for an easier option, you could use plastic blocks – as shown in the techniques section on page 35. If you do this, make sure that you place the blocks so that they are out of the way – well clear of the computer printer and monitor.

Simplifying the design If you want to simplify the design and cut down on the costs, you could miss out the doors.

NEST OF TABLES

A nest of tables is a great idea. Perhaps they don't seem so wonderful when they are just sitting there looking overly complicated, but when the guests arrive they really come into their own. One minute you have a single coffee table and a room full of people looking for somewhere to put their tea and cakes, and the next you have three coffee tables and everyone is happy. Of course, when the tables have superbly smooth lines and are delightfully decorated with inlaid veneer banding, things get better and better. Just in case you have worries about the difficulties of working with banding, you will soon see that it is no more difficult than sticking down a length of masking tape.

YOU WILL NEED

- Jigsaw

- Compound mitre saw

- Drill and 10 mm ($^{13}/_{32}$ in) twist bit with a brad point

- Cordless driver and screwdriver bit to fit your screws

- Router and 12 mm ($^{15}/_{32}$ in) straight cutter

- Orbital sander, 80-grit and 600-grit sandpaper

- 2 G-clamps and 2 sash clamps (or equivalent)

- Scalpel

- Maple:
  A 2 pieces, 940 x 60 x 60 mm (37 x 2⅜ x 2⅜ in)
  B 4 pieces, 400 x 60 x 60 mm (15¾ x 2⅜ x 2⅜ in)
  C 10 pieces, 380 x 60 x 60 mm (14$^{31}/_{32}$ x 2⅜ x 2⅜ in)
  D 8 pieces, 320 x 60 x 60 mm (1$^{19}/_{32}$ x 2⅜ x 2⅜ in)

- Birch plywood:
  E 1 piece, 830 x 390 x 9 mm (32$^{11}/_{16}$ x 15$^{11}/_{32}$ x $^{11}/_{32}$ in)
  F 2 pieces, 390 x 270 x 9 mm (15$^{11}/_{32}$ x 10⅝ x $^{11}/_{32}$ in)

- Decorative banding:
  2 pieces, 820 x 7 x 1.5 mm (32$^{9}/_{32}$ x $^{9}/_{32}$ x $^{1}/_{16}$ in)
  6 pieces, 380 x 7 x 1.5 mm (14$^{31}/_{32}$ x $^{9}/_{32}$ x $^{1}/_{16}$ in)
  4 pieces, 260 x 7 x 1.5 mm (10¼ x $^{9}/_{32}$ x $^{1}/_{16}$ in)

- Fluted dowels: 84 x 10 mm (3$^{5}/_{16}$ x $^{13}/_{32}$ in) in diameter, 40 mm (1$^{9}/_{16}$ in) long

- PVA glue

- Finishing oil

- Cloths for wiping up excess glue and applying oil

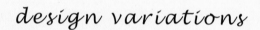

design variations

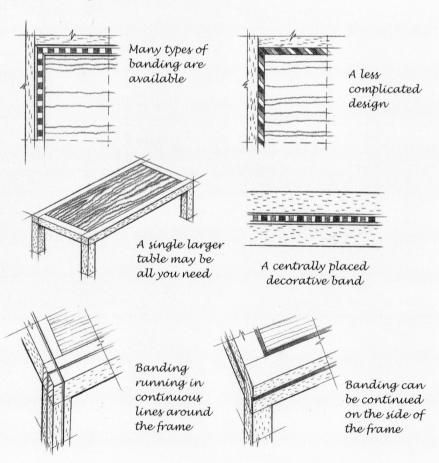

Many types of banding are available

A less complicated design

A single larger table may be all you need

A centrally placed decorative band

Banding running in continuous lines around the frame

Banding can be continued on the side of the frame

Construction time: **3 weekends**

Power tools required: **compound mitre saw, jigsaw, cordless driver, drill, router and orbital sander**

NEST OF TABLES CONSTRUCTION DRAWING

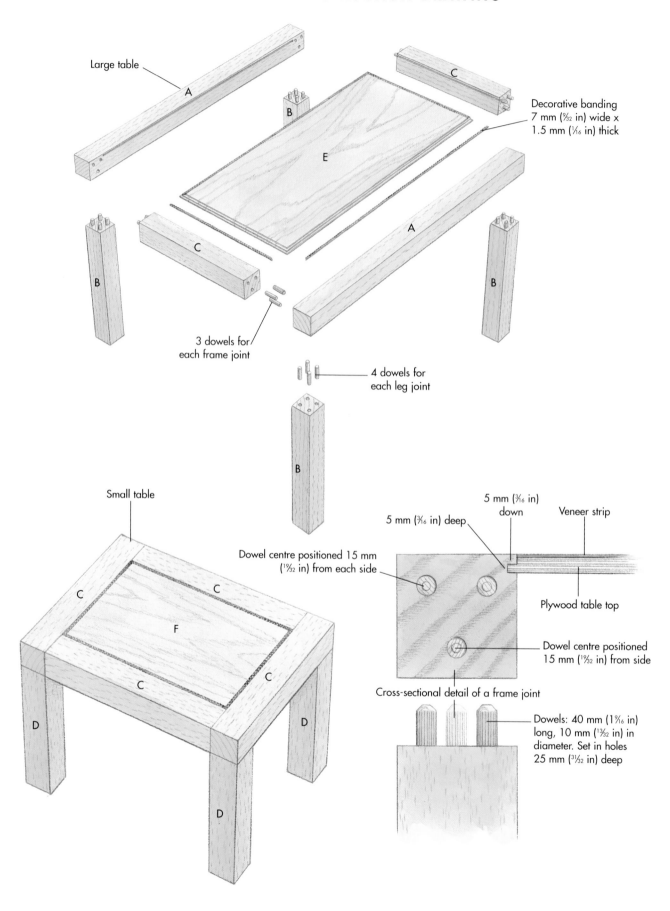

Large table

A

C

Decorative banding
7 mm (%₂ in) wide x
1.5 mm (¹⁄₁₆ in) thick

B

E

A

B

C

B

3 dowels for
each frame joint

4 dowels for
each leg joint

B

Small table

5 mm (³⁄₁₆ in)
down

5 mm (³⁄₁₆ in) deep

Veneer strip

Dowel centre positioned 15 mm
(¹⁹⁄₃₂ in) from each side

C   C

F

Plywood table top

C   C

Dowel centre positioned
15 mm (¹⁹⁄₃₂ in) from side

C

Cross-sectional detail of a frame joint

D   D

Dowels: 40 mm (1⁵⁄₁₆ in)
long, 10 mm (¹³⁄₃₂ in) in
diameter. Set in holes
25 mm (³¹⁄₃₂ in) deep

D

HOW TO BUILD THE NEST OF TABLES

1 Use a pencil, tape measure and square to mark the length of the 12 legs (B) and the 12 rails (A, C), and then cut them to length on the compound mitre saw. Use a 60 x 60 mm (2⅜ x 2⅜ in) offcut (about 40 mm/1⁹⁄₁₆ in long) and plywood offcuts to make the drilling jig as shown above. The centres of the six holes are positioned 15 mm (¹⁹⁄₃₂ in) from the sides.

2 One leg at a time, secure the piece in the vice so that the top end is uppermost, and clamp the jig squarely in place on the top of the leg. Use the drill to bore out four holes (one at each corner). Masking tape wrapped around the drill bit indicates the depth required.

3 One rail at a time, clamp the piece flat on the bench so that the appropriate face is uppermost, and clamp the jig squarely in place. Look at the construction drawings and note which of the holes need to be drilled, then use the drill to bore out the correct pattern of holes.

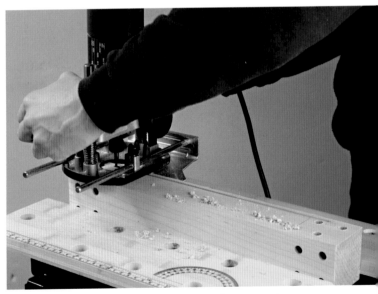

4 One rail at a time, secure the piece in the vice so that the appropriate face is uppermost, and mark the position of the groove. Take the router, set the fence so that the groove is going to be perfectly placed, switch on the power and cut the groove.

5 One piece at a time, clamp the plywood for the table top (E, F) on the bench with its best face uppermost. Take the router, set the fence in place, then switch on the power and make the cut. First cut the inner rebate for the inlaid banding, then the outer tongue.

6 Have a look at the construction drawings and see how the tables fit together. Glue the dowels into the ends of the legs (B, D) and six of the rails (C); apply PVA glue to the inside of the holes and tap in the dowels. Wipe away the excess glue.

7 One table at a time, apply glue to the inside of the remaining dowel holes in the rails (A, C) and fit them together so that they enclose the plywood table top (E, F). Check that the tongue is located in the groove, and clamp up with one clamp at either end. To ensure squareness, make slight adjustments to the clamps until the two diagonal measurements are equal. When the glue has dried, fit the legs (B, D) in place, check for squareness (very important) and clamp up.

8 One table at a time, spread glue in the groove, set the banding in place so that it overlaps at the corners, and secure with masking tape. Mitre the corners by cutting right through the overlap with a scalpel or craft knife. When the glue has dried, remove the tape and sand the tables all over to a smooth finish. Complete the tables by applying oil.

TIPS AND TROUBLESHOOTING

Plywood table tops   You could cut down on the work by not rebating the edge of the plywood. Instead, you could fix it with plastic blocks.

Mortise-and-tenon joints   If you enjoy cutting joints by hand, you could miss out the dowels and fit the legs with mortise-and-tenon joints.

Fixing the dowels   When you are using the hammer to tap the dowels into place, make sure that you don't snap them off or knock them out of shape.

STORAGE STOOL

This is one of those ideas that just grew and grew. One moment we wanted no more than a humble little footstool – somewhere to put our feet up when watching TV – and the next we were considering all sorts of cushion and storage options. At the end of the day, we settled for a neat and plain design, with a ready-made cushion and a sliding drawer. We particularly like the drawer with the metal runners, and the chance to use cam dowel fixings. There are many possibilities. If you look at the design variations, you will see that you could have a different arrangement of drawers, a custom-made padded top that sits over a hidden storage well, a cushion sitting in a recess, and so on.

YOU WILL NEED

- Jigsaw
- Compound mitre saw
- Biscuit jointer and 8 x No. 20 biscuits
- Drill, twist bits and forstner bit to suit cam dowels
- Cordless driver and screwdriver bit to fit your screws
- Orbital sander, 80-grit and 600-grit sandpaper
- 2 G-clamps and 2 sash clamps
- Pin hammer
- Birch plywood:
  A 1 piece, 495 x 495 x 25.5 mm (19½ x 19½ x 1 in)
  B 3 pieces, 355 x 215 x 17.5 mm (13³¹⁄₃₂ x 8¹⁵⁄₃₂ x ¹¹⁄₁₆ in)
  F 1 piece, 350 x 210 x 17.5 mm (13²⁵⁄₃₂ x 8⁹⁄₃₂ x ¹¹⁄₁₆ in)
  I 1 piece, 392 x 273 x 4.5 mm (15⁷⁄₁₆ x 10¾ x ³⁄₁₆ in)
- Maple:
  A1 2 pieces, 505 x 25.5 x 5 mm (19⅞ x 1 x ³⁄₁₆ in)
  A2 2 pieces, 495 x 25.5 x 5 mm (19½ x 1 x ³⁄₁₆ in)
  C 4 pieces, 265 x 50 x 50 mm (10⁷⁄₁₆ x 1³¹⁄₃₂ x 1³¹⁄₃₂ in)
- Pine:
  D 2 pieces, 410 x 25 x 18 mm (16⁵⁄₃₂ x ³¹⁄₃₂ x ²³⁄₃₂ in)
  E 2 pieces, 410 x 33 x 18 mm (16⁵⁄₃₂ x 1½ x ²³⁄₃₂ in)
  G 2 pieces, 400 x 145 x 18 mm (15¾ x 5²⁹⁄₃₂ x ²³⁄₃₂ in)
  H 1 piece, 263 x 150 x 18 mm (10¹¹⁄₃₂ x 5²⁹⁄₃₂ x ²³⁄₃₂ in)
- 12 cam dowel fixings
- 2 metal drawer runners with screws
- Veneer pins
- Crossheaded screws: 8 x No. 8, 40 mm (1⁹⁄₁₆ in) long
- Wood-coloured filler
- PVA glue
- Danish oil
- Cloths for wiping up excess glue and applying oil

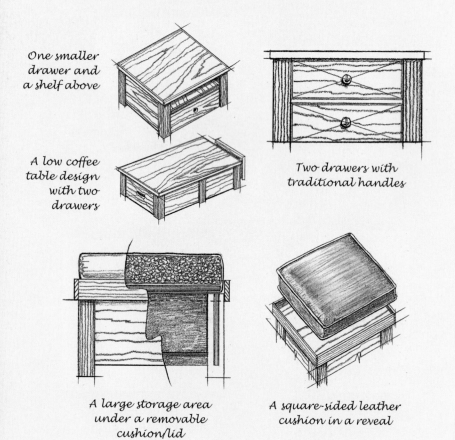

design variations

One smaller drawer and a shelf above

A low coffee table design with two drawers

Two drawers with traditional handles

A large storage area under a removable cushion/lid

A square-sided leather cushion in a reveal

Construction time: 1 weekend

Power tools required: jigsaw, compound mitre saw, biscuit jointer, cordless driver, drill and orbital sander

STORAGE STOOL CONSTRUCTION DRAWING

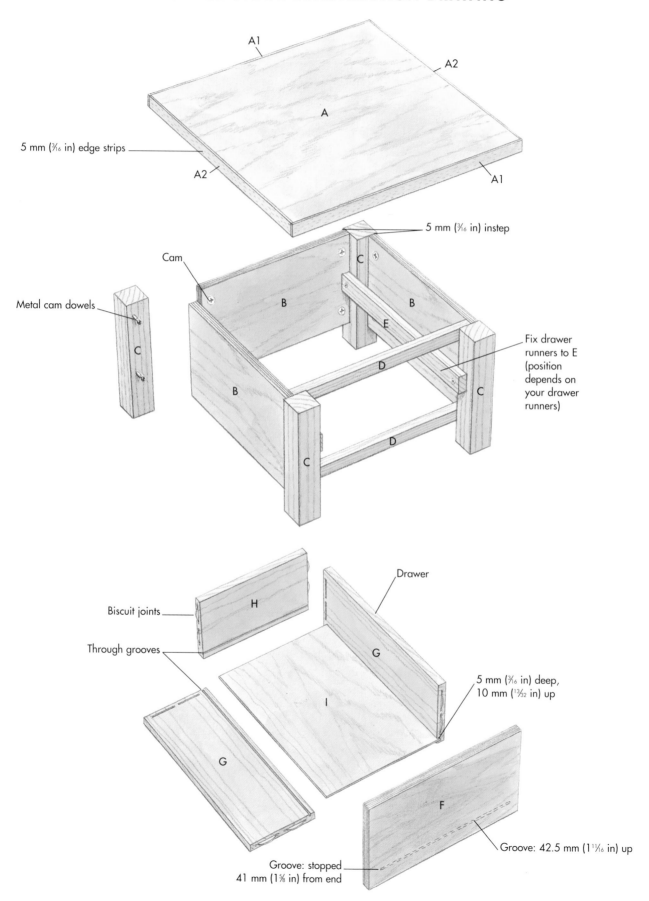

A1

A2

A

5 mm (³⁄₁₆ in) edge strips

A2

A1

5 mm (³⁄₁₆ in) instep

Cam

C

Metal cam dowels

B

B

C

E

Fix drawer runners to E (position depends on your drawer runners)

B

D

B

C

D

C

Drawer

Biscuit joints

H

Through grooves

G

G

5 mm (³⁄₁₆ in) deep, 10 mm (¹³⁄₃₂ in) up

I

G

F

Groove: stopped 41 mm (1⅝ in) from end

Groove: 42.5 mm (1¹¹⁄₁₆ in) up

HOW TO BUILD THE STORAGE STOOL

1 Use a pencil, tape measure and square to establish the length of the four legs (C). Cut the legs to length and carefully mark in the position of the metal cam dowels. Drill pilot holes and screw the metal dowels in place so that you have four dowels on each of the two back legs, and two dowels on each of the front legs.

2 Take the three plywood boards for the sides (B) and back of the stool (B), and mark the position of the large cam holes on the face of the ply, and the small holes on the end edge. Use the forstner bit to bore the large cam holes, and then a twist bit to drill the dowel holes that run into the cam holes.

3 Slide the side boards in place on the metal dowels. Then, one fixing at a time, set the metal cam in the hole so that it is located on the dowel, and use the screwdriver to tighten up. The act of turning the cam will clench the joint up tightly. Repeat this procedure with all the cam dowel fixings.

4 Mark in the position of the two front rails (D) and the two drawer runner rails (E), and screw them in place. Make sure that the front rails are flush with the top and bottom edges of the plywood sides (B), and that the runners are aligned with each other and parallel with the overall frame.

5 Take the pieces that go to make the drawer – the three sides (G, H), the front (F) and the base (I) – and mark in the position of the grooves and slots. Cut the grooves and slots with the biscuit jointer. Glue the biscuits in place, set the whole thing together, check that the plywood base is located properly, and clamp up.

6 Use the pencil and tape measure to mark in the precise position of the metal drawer runners. Screw the metal runners in place on the wooden runner rails (E), double-check your measurements, and screw the other halves of the runners on the sides of the drawers (G). Check the action and make necessary adjustments.

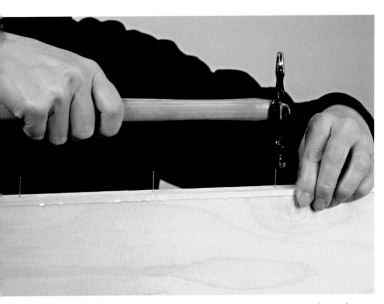

7 Take the strips of maple (A1, A2) and glue and pin them on the exposed edges of the plywood stool top (A). Knock the pinheads below the surface of the wood and fill the holes with wood-coloured filler. Finally, sand all the surfaces to a smooth finish and give them a couple of coats of Danish oil.

TIPS AND TROUBLESHOOTING

Cushion and sizing If you are using a ready-made cushion, it's a good idea to start by getting the cushion. You can then adjust the overall size of the stool to fit the cushion. If you are having a cushion custom made, it's better to go for a boxed cushion.

Fitting the cushion You could tack the cushion to the stool so that it is a permanent fixture – so that you finish up with an upholstered stool.

Making the drawers with dowels If you don't have, or don't want to use a biscuit jointer, you could modify the design and make the drawer using wooden fluted dowels.

Metal drawer runners You could cut costs and make the drawer runners from thin strips of wood.

TV UNIT

No more trailing wires and flapping doors – now you can have this beautifully designed, custom-made TV unit complete with tambour doors. A tambour is a sliding door on a desk, cupboard or other item that is made of thin strips of wood glued side by side on to a canvas backing. I don't know about the origins of the name, but it seems to refer to items or structures that are drum-like, curved or round in form. Once in place, a tambour door presents itself as a smooth surface. To open our pair of doors, you simply hold the two handles and draw them apart, and then watch as the doors quietly vanish into the sides of the cabinet.

design variations

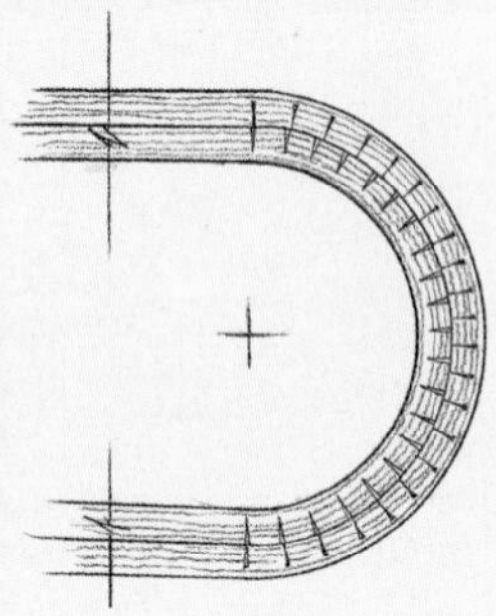

A cross-sectional detail showing how numerous saw cuts can be used to create a permanently curved shape

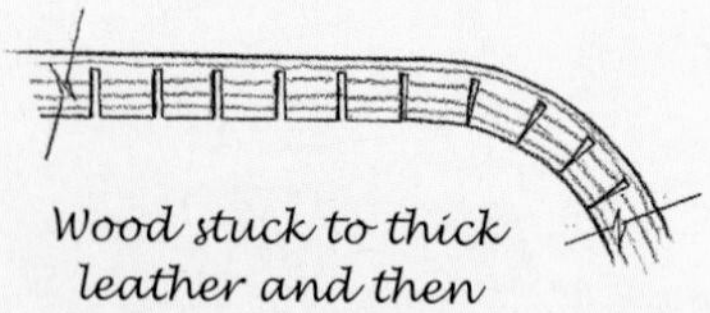

Wood stuck to thick leather and then sawn through with repeated saw cuts (leaving leather intact) might make a good tambour

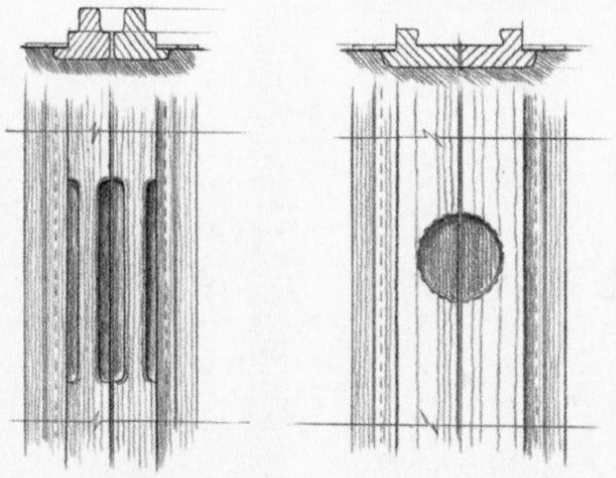

Drawer handle variations made from solid wood (cross-sectional details are shown above)

YOU WILL NEED

- Compasses
- Jigsaw
- Compound mitre saw
- Drill, twist bits and forstner bit to suit cam dowels, and hole saw
- Cordless driver and screwdriver bit to fit your screws
- Router and 6 mm ($\frac{1}{4}$ in) and 12 mm ($\frac{15}{32}$ in) straight cutters
- Orbital sander, 80-grit and 600-grit sandpaper
- 2 G-clamps and 2 sash clamps
- Pin hammer
- Electric iron
- Birch plywood:
  A 2 pieces, 976 x 604 x 25.5 mm ($38\frac{3}{8}$ x $23\frac{25}{32}$ x 1 in)
  B 2 pieces, 930 x 516 x 17 mm ($36\frac{5}{8}$ x $20\frac{5}{16}$ x $\frac{21}{32}$ in)
  C 2 pieces, 790 x 511 x 17 mm ($31\frac{3}{32}$ x $20\frac{1}{8}$ x $\frac{21}{32}$ in)
  D 1 piece, 506 x 156 x 17 mm ($19\frac{29}{32}$ x $6\frac{5}{32}$ x $\frac{21}{32}$ in)
  E 1 piece, 506 x 206 x 17 mm ($19\frac{29}{32}$ x $8\frac{1}{8}$ x $\frac{21}{32}$ in)
  F 2 pieces, 930 x 502 x 9.5 mm ($36\frac{5}{8}$ x $19\frac{3}{4}$ x $\frac{3}{8}$ in)
  G 1 piece, 930 x 824 x 4.5 mm ($36\frac{5}{8}$ x $32\frac{7}{16}$ x $\frac{3}{16}$ in)
- Maple:
  H 44 pieces, 940 x 23.5 x 9.5 mm (37 x $\frac{15}{16}$ x $\frac{3}{8}$ in)
  B1 2 pieces, 930 x 17 x 5 mm ($36\frac{5}{8}$ x $\frac{21}{32}$ x $\frac{3}{16}$ in)
  C1 2 pieces, 790 x 17 x 5 mm ($31\frac{3}{32}$ x $\frac{21}{32}$ x $\frac{3}{16}$ in)
  D1 1 piece, 156 x 17 x 5 mm ($6\frac{5}{32}$ x $\frac{21}{32}$ x $\frac{3}{16}$ in)
  E1 1 piece, 206 x 17 x 5 mm ($8\frac{1}{8}$ x $\frac{21}{32}$ x $\frac{3}{16}$ in)
  F1 2 pieces, 930 x 9.5 x 5 mm ($36\frac{5}{8}$ x $\frac{3}{8}$ x $\frac{3}{16}$ in)
- Canvas:
  2 pieces, 920 x 525 mm ($43\frac{7}{32}$ x $20\frac{21}{32}$ in)
- Plywood for template (size depends on your router, see step 5)
- Birch veneer edge strip:
  A1 2 pieces, 2100 x 25.5 mm ($82\frac{11}{16}$ x 1 in)
- Fluted dowels: 8 x 6 mm ($\frac{1}{4}$ in) in diameter, 30 mm ($1\frac{3}{16}$ in) long
- Veneer pins
- Crossheaded screws: 12 x No. 6, 20 mm ($\frac{25}{32}$ in) long
- Handles of your choice
- 4 swivelling castors with wheels 70 mm ($2\frac{3}{4}$ in) in diameter and 20 mm ($\frac{25}{32}$ in) screws to fit
- Wood-coloured filler
- PVA glue
- Danish oil
- Cloths for wiping up excess glue and applying oil

Construction time: **3 weekends**

Power tools required: **jigsaw, cordless driver, compound mitre saw, drill, router and orbital sander**

TV UNIT CONSTRUCTION DRAWING

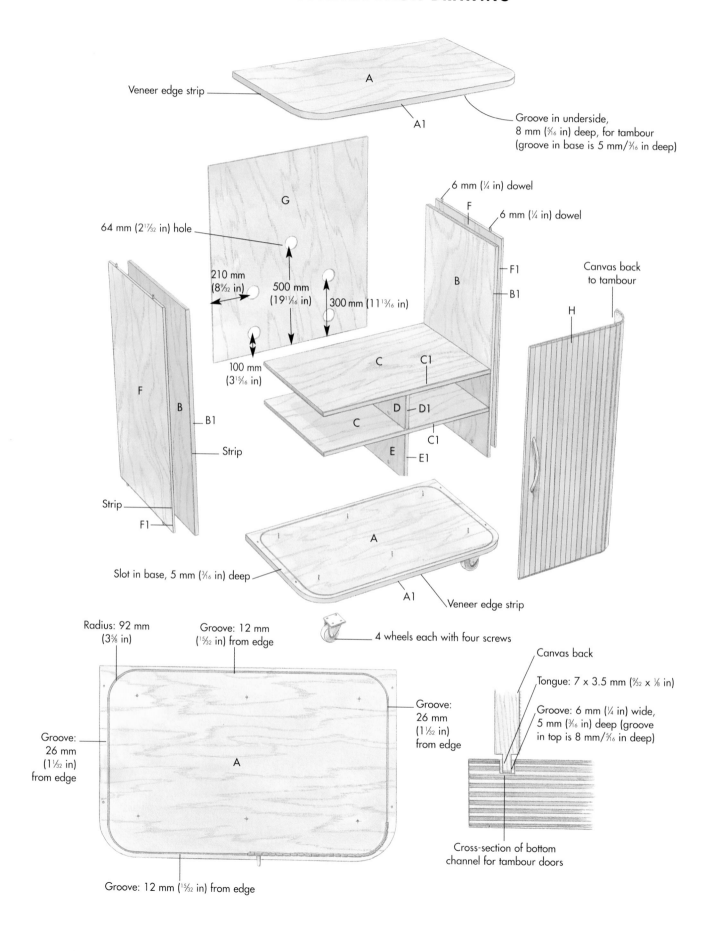

Veneer edge strip

A1

A

Groove in underside,
8 mm (⁵⁄₁₆ in) deep, for tambour
(groove in base is 5 mm/³⁄₁₆ in deep)

G

6 mm (¼ in) dowel

F

6 mm (¼ in) dowel

64 mm (2¹⁷⁄₃₂ in) hole

210 mm
(8⁵⁄₃₂ in)

500 mm
(19¹¹⁄₁₆ in)

300 mm (11¹³⁄₁₆ in)

100 mm
(3¹⁵⁄₁₆ in)

F1

B

B1

Canvas back
to tambour

H

F

B

B1

Strip

C

C1

Strip

C

D   D1

A

E

E1

C1

F1

Slot in base, 5 mm (³⁄₁₆ in) deep

A1

Veneer edge strip

Radius: 92 mm
(3⅝ in)

Groove: 12 mm
(¹⁵⁄₃₂ in) from edge

4 wheels each with four screws

Canvas back

Tongue: 7 x 3.5 mm (⁹⁄₃₂ x ⅛ in)

Groove:
26 mm
(1¹⁄₃₂ in)
from edge

Groove:
26 mm
(1¹⁄₃₂ in)
from edge

A

Groove: 6 mm (¼ in) wide,
5 mm (³⁄₁₆ in) deep (groove
in top is 8 mm/⁵⁄₁₆ in deep)

Cross-section of bottom
channel for tambour doors

Groove: 12 mm (¹⁵⁄₃₂ in) from edge

HOW TO BUILD THE TV UNIT

1 Use a pencil, tape measure and square to establish the size of the various pieces of plywood (A–G). Cut them out with the jigsaw. Fix the strips of maple (B1, C1, D1, E1, F1), to the edges of the sides and shelves using glue and pins. Knock the pinheads below the surface of the wood and fill the holes with filler. Give everything an initial sanding.

2 Use a pencil, tape measure and square to carefully mark the positions of the metal cam dowels – the cam holes on the face of the ply, and the dowel holes on edges and faces.

3 Check the marking out, and use twist bits to bore holes for the dowels – pilot holes in the face for the screw end, and deep holes in the edge for the shaft. Use the forstner bit to bore the large cam holes. Make sure that the shaft and cam holes are aligned and centred one to another.

4 Use the hole saw to cut the pattern of holes in the board that goes to make the back of the unit (G). Rest the workpiece on a piece of scrap wood and proceed slowly to avoid splintering the wood.

5 Take the top and bottom boards (A) and mark in the position and extent of the grooves for the tambour doors. Cut the plywood template to size and shape, and pin it in place on the face to be worked. Fit the 6 mm (¼ in) cutter in the router, set it down so that the round part of the base can run up against the template, and then cut the groove.

6 Remove the template. Take the iron-on strips of flexible veneer, and iron them in place on the edges of the top and bottom boards. Sand the edge of the veneer to a good fit and finish.

7 Make a routing jig for rebating the tambour strips (H) using offcuts, as shown above (measurements depend on your router). Fit the router with the 12 mm (¹⁵⁄₃₂ in) straight cutter and make one or two passes to cut a rebate. Repeat this procedure on both ends and both faces, until you have achieved the top and bottom tongues.

8 Set the strips for the tambour side by side in the same jig used in Step 7, spread PVA glue over the surfaces and allow to dry. Dampen the canvas, pin it down to a smooth surface, apply a coat of PVA glue and allow to dry. Place the canvas (glue-side down) on the tambour strips in the jig and use the iron to melt the glue and stick the fabric to the wood.

9 Perform a trial fitting. Slide the side boards in place on the metal dowels, slide the tambour doors in place, then, one fixing at a time, set the metal cam in the hole so that it is located on the dowel, and use the screwdriver to tighten up. The act of turning the cam will clench the joint up tightly. Repeat this procedure with all the cam dowel fixings.

10 Check that the joints have all closed up and that the doors slide smoothly, and make adjustments if necessary. Take the unit apart and use the sander and the 600-grit sandpaper to rub all the surfaces to a smoother finish. Give all the surfaces a couple of coats of Danish oil. Attach the swivelling castors and door handles, and reassemble the components. Rub candle wax (colourless wax) into the door grooves so that the doors will slide more easily.

WINE GLASS TRAY

This intricately constructed tray was inspired by a little Georgian silver tray that my aged aunt had in her house. It is an elegant solution to the problem of how to carry six wine glasses – either full or empty. Of course, if you like the overall concept, but are not so keen on the details, there is no reason why you cannot change things around to suit your own taste and needs. You could make it much larger, say for twelve glasses, or leave out the little finial balls. You could paint it, or have more or fewer rails. You could even make the rails from stainless-steel rods: there are lots of exciting possibilities.

YOU WILL NEED

- Compasses
- Jigsaw
- Compound mitre saw
- Biscuit jointer and 12 x No. 20 biscuits
- Drill press and 6 mm (¼ in) twist bit with a brad point
- Router, 12 mm (¹⁵⁄₃₂ in) straight cutter, 6 mm (¼ in) radius cutter and template guide (see step 4)
- Orbital sander, 80-grit and 600-grit sandpaper
- Palm sander
- 2 G-clamps
- Maple:
  A 3 pieces, 448 x 105 x 17.5 mm (17⅝ x 4⅛ x ¹¹⁄₁₆ in)
  B 12 pieces, 173 x 20 x 20 mm (6²⁵⁄₃₂ x ²⁵⁄₃₂ x ²⁵⁄₃₂ in)
- Dowel for rods:
  C 51 pieces, 6 mm (¼ in) in diameter and 120.5 mm (4¾ in) long
- Wooden eggs/balls/beads:
  D 12 pieces, approximately 20 mm (²⁵⁄₃₂ in) in diameter
- Fluted dowels: 24 x 6 mm (¼ in) in diameter, 30 mm (1³⁄₁₆ in) long
- PVA glue
- Finishing oil
- Cloths for wiping up excess glue and applying oil

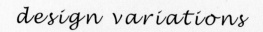

design variations

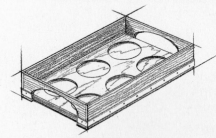

A less complicated construction may be more appealing

Simplified and with rounded corner details

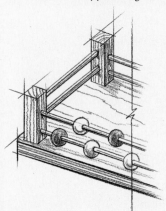

Balls threaded on to dowels could decorate the sides

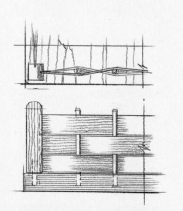

Thin slats slotted into corner posts and woven around the dowels (a plan view is shown above)

Construction time: 2 weekends

Power tools required: jigsaw, biscuit jointer, router, compound mitre saw, drill press, orbital sander and palm sander

WINE GLASS TRAY CONSTRUCTION DRAWING

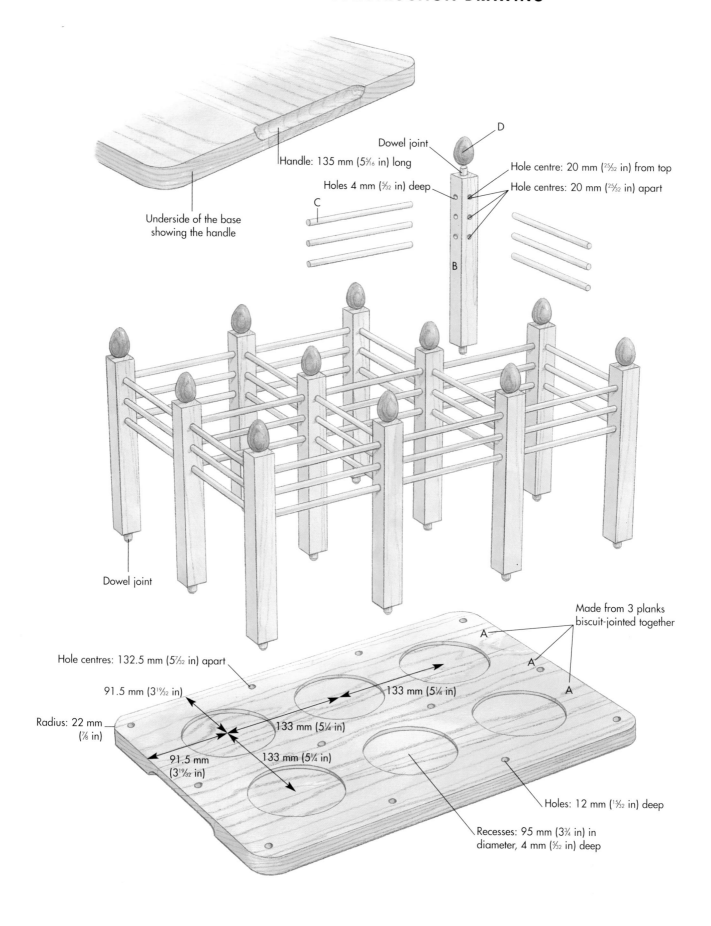

Handle: 135 mm (5⁵⁄₁₆ in) long

Underside of the base
showing the handle

Dowel joint

D

Hole centre: 20 mm (²⁵⁄₃₂ in) from top

Holes 4 mm (⁵⁄₃₂ in) deep

Hole centres: 20 mm (²⁵⁄₃₂ in) apart

C

B

Dowel joint

Made from 3 planks
biscuit-jointed together

A

A

A

Hole centres: 132.5 mm (5⁷⁄₃₂ in) apart

91.5 mm (3¹⁹⁄₃₂ in)

133 mm (5¼ in)

133 mm (5¼ in)

Radius: 22 mm
(⅞ in)

133 mm (5¼ in)

91.5 mm
(3¹⁹⁄₃₂ in)

Holes: 12 mm (¹⁵⁄₃₂ in) deep

Recesses: 95 mm (3¾ in) in
diameter, 4 mm (⁵⁄₃₂ in) deep

HOW TO BUILD THE WINE GLASS TRAY

1 Cut the 'tray' wood (A) to length (allow an extra 15 mm (¹⁹⁄₃₂ in) or so at each end – this will be cut off in step 2). Use a pencil, tape measure and square to establish the position of the biscuit slots. Use the jointer to cut the biscuit slots in the three main boards. Dribble PVA glue in the slots, tap the biscuits home, put the three boards together and clamp up.

2 Use a pencil, ruler and compass to draw the shape of the tray on the slab. Cut out the profile with the jigsaw and sand it to a smooth, round-cornered finish. Establish which you consider to be the best face, then draw in the position of the handles on what will be the underside.

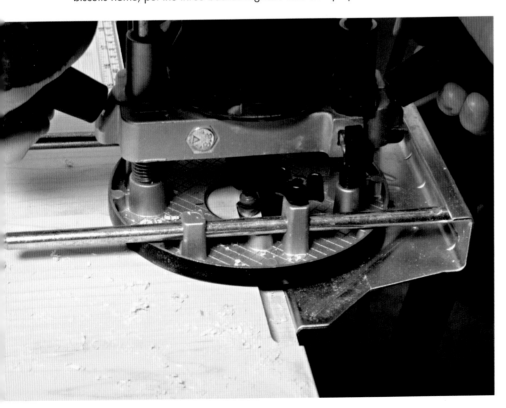

3 Clamp the workpiece to the bench, fit the router with the radius cutter, and rout the coved handles on the underside of both ends. Use the two grades of sandpaper to make the handle shapes smooth. Turn the board over and mark the positions of the hole centres for the dowel joints. Use the drill press and the 6 mm (¼ in) twist bit to make holes 12 mm (¹⁵⁄₃₂ in) deep.

4 Mark the position of the six recesses and make a routing template to suit your template guide as shown above (a template guide is usually supplied with the router; it fixes to the base, encircles the cutter and provides a 'bush' for following a template). Use dowels and the holes made in step 3 to locate the template. Rout in a clockwise direction.

5 Take the compound mitre saw and set the end stop for the length of the square-section posts (B). To cut the posts, slide the wood hard up against the fence and the stop, and make the cut. Cut all 12 posts to length, and then change the stop length and cut the 51 dowels (C) (use an offcut to hold the dowels and keep your hands away from the blade).

6 Have a look at the construction drawings, and see how the square-section posts fall into three groups: four posts with rod holes on two faces, six posts with rod holes on three faces, and two posts with rod holes on four faces. As shown, make a drilling jig using an offcut and a nail. Clamp the jig in place to suit one of the hole positions and drill all the posts as necessary. Repeat the procedure for the other two hole positions.

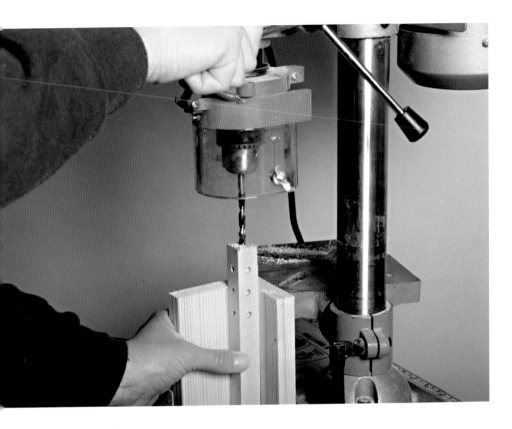

7 Make another jig (using offcuts as shown) for drilling the holes in the ends of the posts. Clamp the jig in place on the drill press, and set the depth stop for drilling holes about 17 mm (²¹⁄₃₂ in) deep. One post at a time, set the post in the jig and drill a dowel hole in each end of all 12 posts.

8 Make another jig (using an offcut as shown) for drilling the holes in the eggs/balls/beads (D). The eggs/balls/beads need to wedge tightly in the hole in the jig. Clamp the jig in place on the drill press, and set the depth stop for drilling holes about 12 mm (¹⁵⁄₃₂ in) deep. Carefully drill all 12 holes.

9 Perform a trial run assembly. Then dribble a small amount of PVA glue in all dowel and rod holes, push the fluted dowels into the ends of the posts, push the rods in place in the posts, and set the posts in place on the tray. Finally, sand to a good finish and wipe over with oil.

HOPE CHEST

This hope or dower chest draws its inspiration from the simple folk-art chests made by German settlers in America between 1750 and 1850. Chests of this type and size are characterized by having an architectural façade made up of arches supported on capitals and pilasters, a fretted plinth that shows a cyma curve, and by being flat-painted in bright primary colours and decorated with stylized birds and flower imagery. While our project stays close to the spirit of the original chest, we have nudged the design so that it can be made with a few basic power tools.

design variations

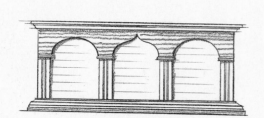

A pointed arch and applied mouldings at the base

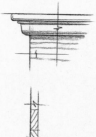

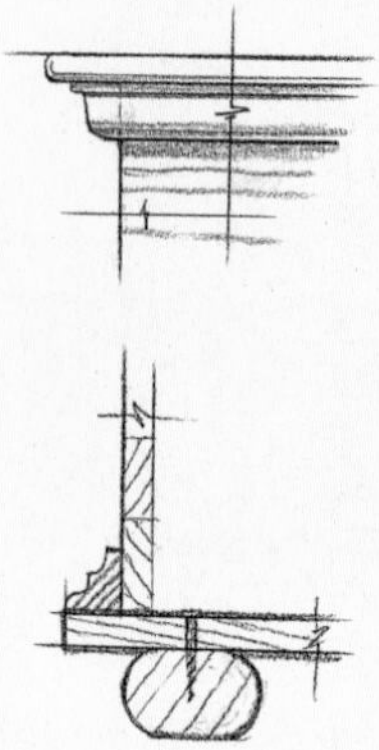

A moulding fitted to the underside of the lid

Cross-sectional drawing showing moulding and foot detail

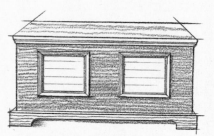

Square panels with mitred mouldings can be applied to the front

YOU WILL NEED

- Compasses

- Jigsaw

- Compound mitre saw

- Cordless driver, screwdriver bit to fit your screws and counter-bore bit

- Router and 6 mm (¼ in) round-over cutter with a bearing tip

- Orbital sander and 80-grit sandpaper

- 2 G-clamps

- Pin hammer

- Pine block board:
  A 2 pieces, 950 x 490 x 19 mm (37¹³⁄₃₂ x 19⁹⁄₃₂ x ¾ in)
  B 2 pieces, 889 x 300 x 18 mm (35 x 11¹³⁄₁₆ x ²³⁄₃₂ in)
  C 2 pieces, 410 x 300 x 18 mm (16⁵⁄₃₂ x 11¹³⁄₁₆ x ²³⁄₃₂ in)

- Pine:
  D 4 pieces, 300 x 32 x 32 mm (11¹³⁄₁₆ x 1¼ x 1¼ in)
  E 2 pieces, 814 x 32 x 32 mm (20¹⁄₃₂ x 1¼ x 1¼ in)
  F 2 pieces, 375 x 32 x 32 mm (14¾ x 1¼ x 1¼ in)
  G 4 pieces, 145 x 32 x 32 mm (5²³⁄₃₂ x 1¼ x 1¼ in)
  H 1 piece, 914 x 145 x 18 mm (35³¹⁄₃₂ x 5²³⁄₃₂ x ²³⁄₃₂ in)
  I 1 piece, 878 x 145 x 18 mm (34⁹⁄₁₆ x 5²³⁄₃₂ x ²³⁄₃₂ in)
  J 2 pieces, 457 x 145 x 18 mm (18 x 5²³⁄₃₂ x ²³⁄₃₂ in)
  K 1 piece, 889 x 68 x 18 mm (35 x 2¹¹⁄₁₆ x ²³⁄₃₂ in)
  L 4 pieces, 200 x 70 x 18 mm (7⅞ x 2¾ x ²³⁄₃₂ in)
  M 2 pieces, 85 x 32 x 32 mm (3¹¹⁄₃₂ x 1¼ x 1¼ in)
  N 2 pieces, 79 x 32 x 32 mm (3⅛ x 1¼ x 1¼ in)
  Q 2 pieces, 346 x 70 x 18 mm (13⅝ x 2¾ x ²³⁄₃₂ in)

- Ridged section moulding:
  O 2 pieces, 68 x 30 x 6 mm (2¹¹⁄₁₆ x 1³⁄₁₆ x ¼ in)
  P 2 pieces, 71 x 30 x 6 mm (2²⁵⁄₃₂ x 1³⁄₁₆ x ¼ in)

- Veneer pins

- Crossheaded screws: 90 x No. 8, 40 mm (1⁹⁄₁₆ in) long

- 2 x 15 mm (¹⁹⁄₃₂ in) butt hinges with screws

- Wood-coloured filler

- PVA glue

- Paint of your choice

- Paintbrush

- Cloth for wiping up excess glue

Construction time: 2 weekends

Power tools required: jigsaw, compound mitre saw, cordless driver, router and orbital sander

HOPE CHEST CONSTRUCTION DRAWING

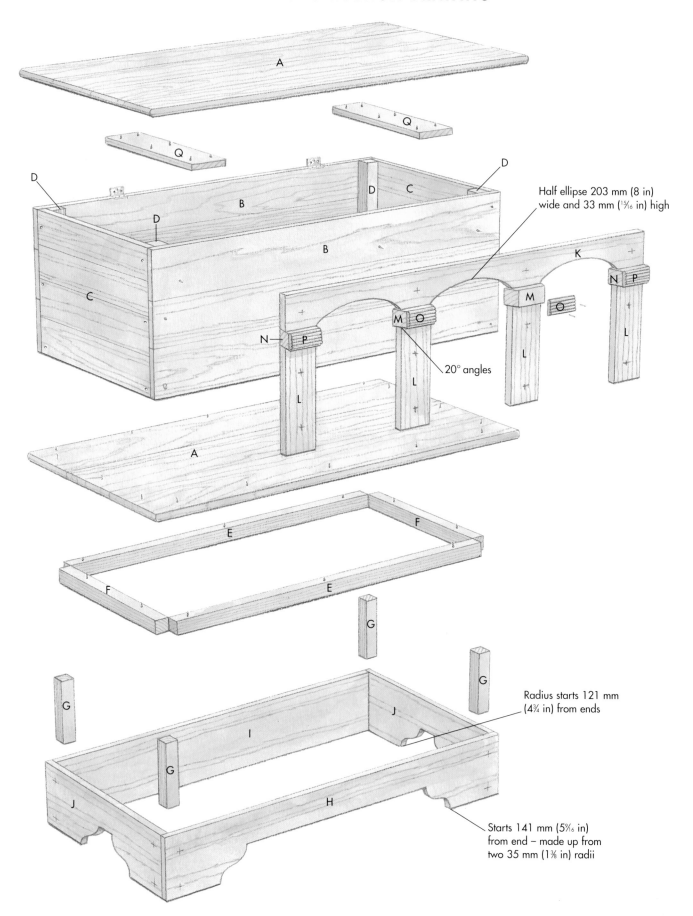

Half ellipse 203 mm (8 in) wide and 33 mm (1⁵⁄₁₆ in) high

20° angles

Radius starts 121 mm (4¾ in) from ends

Starts 141 mm (5⁵⁄₁₆ in) from end – made up from two 35 mm (1⅜ in) radii

HOW TO BUILD THE HOPE CHEST

1 Cut all the components to size using the jigsaw for the block board sheets (A, B, C) and the compound mitre saw for the other planks and sticks (D–Q). Counter-bore the fixing points on the front and back panels (B).

2 Position and clamp the front board (B) to its pair of battens (D) so that the battens are on the inside face of the box and set back from the edge by the thickness of an end board (C). Check that everything is square, and screw the battens in place. Repeat this procedure with the back board (B).

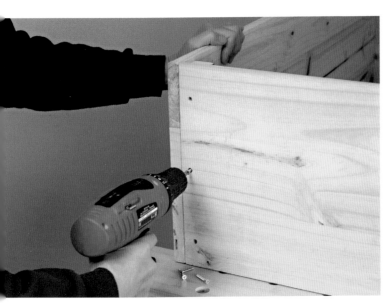

3 Set the front (B) and end boards (C) together so that the outside faces are flush and the corners square, and fix them with screws running from the end boards through to the support battens. Repeat this procedure for all four boards that go to make the sides of the box.

4 Screw the two support battens (Q) to the underside of the lid board (A). Clamp the lid to the workbench so that the underside is uppermost, and use the router to run a curve around the edge. Repeat this procedure on the other side of the board, so that you finish up with a smooth, round nosing.

PERGOLA

One of the swiftest ways of creating a bold statement in your garden is to build a pergola. One moment you have a gateway, a path or a gap in a hedge, for example, and the next you have a feature that draws the eye. Once the pergola is in place, it can be used to support plants, to hang a gate, or as a bower-type structure over a seat … there are many possibilities. Our pergola draws its inspiration from a range of sources. The lattice looks a little French, the cross-members look slightly Chinese and the corner braces or brackets are reminiscent of those seen on English medieval timber-framed buildings.

YOU WILL NEED

- Compasses
- Jigsaw
- Compound mitre saw
- Drill and twist bit to suit your screws
- Cordless driver and screwdriver bit to fit your screws
- Orbital sander and 80-grit sandpaper
- 2 G-clamps
- Tenon saw
- Rubber mallet
- Pine:
  A 8 pieces, 2070 x 70 x 45 mm (81½ x 2¾ x 1²⁵⁄₃₂ in)
  B 16 pieces, 155 x 70 x 45 mm (6³⁄₃₂ x 2¾ x 1²⁵⁄₃₂ in)
  C 2 pieces, 1675 x 100 x 45 mm (65¹⁵⁄₁₆ x 3¹⁵⁄₁₆ x 1²⁵⁄₃₂ in)
  D 4 pieces, 1560 x 100 x 45 mm (61¹³⁄₃₂ x 36¹⁵⁄₁₆ x 1²⁵⁄₃₂ in)
  E 4 pieces, 581 x 100 x 45 mm (22⅞ x 3¹⁵⁄₁₆ x 1²⁵⁄₃₂ in)
- Trellis:
  F 2 pieces, 1857 x 610 mm (73⅛ x 24¹⁄₆₄ in)
- Crossheaded screws:
  12 x No. 8, 40 mm (1⁹⁄₁₆ in) long, and 84 x No. 10, 75 mm (2¹⁵⁄₁₆ in) long
- PVA glue
- Paint/preservative of your choice
- Paintbrush
- Cloth for wiping up excess glue

design variations

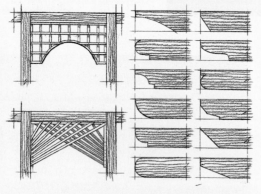

The front of the pergola could be decorated with a lattice archway instead of the angled corner braces

There are many shapes that could be used to finish off the beam ends

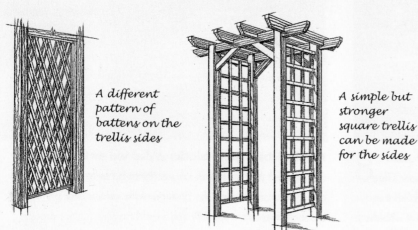

A different pattern of battens on the trellis sides

A simple but stronger square trellis can be made for the sides

Construction time: 3 weekends

Power tools required: compound mitre saw, jigsaw, drill, cordless driver and orbital sander

PERGOLA CONSTRUCTION DRAWING

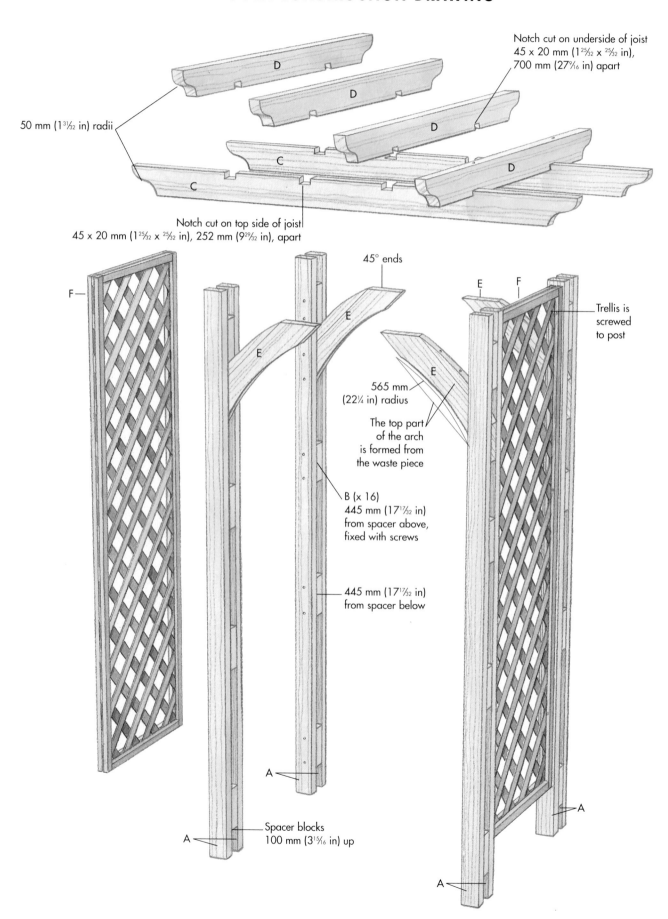

Notch cut on underside of joist 45 x 20 mm (1²⁵⁄₃₂ x ²⁵⁄₃₂ in), 700 mm (27⁹⁄₁₆ in) apart

50 mm (1³¹⁄₃₂ in) radii

Notch cut on top side of joist 45 x 20 mm (1²⁵⁄₃₂ x ²⁵⁄₃₂ in), 252 mm (9²⁹⁄₃₂ in), apart

45° ends

Trellis is screwed to post

565 mm (22¼ in) radius

The top part of the arch is formed from the waste piece

B (x 16) 445 mm (17¹⁷⁄₃₂ in) from spacer above, fixed with screws

445 mm (17¹⁷⁄₃₂ in) from spacer below

Spacer blocks 100 mm (3¹⁵⁄₁₆ in) up

HOW TO BUILD THE PERGOLA

1 Use a hand saw, compound mitre saw or large jigsaw to cut all the components to length – eight main posts (A), two main cross-beams (C), four joists (D) and 16 spacer blocks (B). Use the main beam to position the spacer blocks in relation to the ends of the posts.

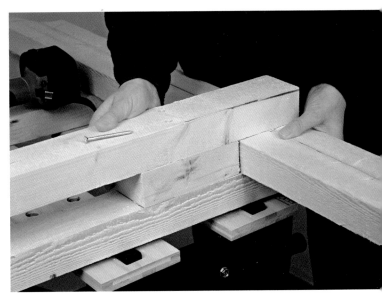

2 Set a post section (A) across a pair of workbenches and screw the spacer blocks (B) in place. Position the second post section (A) so that the blocks are sandwiched, and screw it in place. Position the screws so that they run through different parts of the blocks.

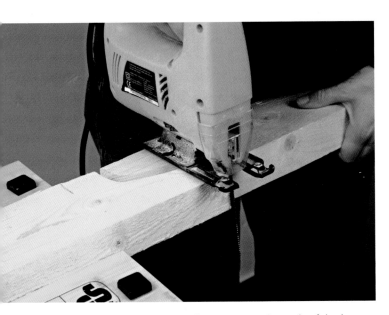

3 Draw the symmetrical 'S' curve on the ends of the beams (C) and joists (D), and cut it through with the jigsaw. **Note:** if you can obtain long enough sections, you could save on costs and time by making the 'S' cut to cut two components from a single piece.

4 Mark out the size and position of the notches – four on the top of each beam (C) and two on the underside of each joist (D) – and cut them out with the jigsaw. Clear each notch with four cuts – two cuts to fix the depth, one curved cut to clear half of the waste, and a final cut to clear the rest.

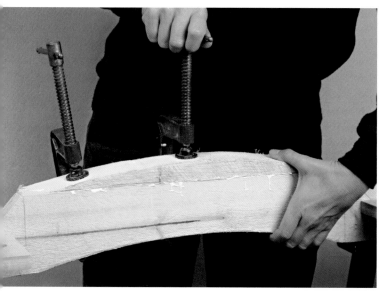

5 One piece at a time, take the sections that you have cut for the curved brackets (E), draw out the shape of the curve, and cut it out with the jigsaw. Take the cut-away segment and glue, clamp and screw it in place on the other side of the section, so that you finish up with a curved section.

6 Set two posts (A) flat on the ground and link them with a cross-beam (C) so that the beam passes through the mortise-like space at the top of the beam. Repeat this procedure with the other two posts and cross-beam. You might need to ease one or more of the screws that run into the spacer blocks.

7 Stand the two post-and-beam frames side by side, and link them by locating the notches on the underside of the joists (D) with the notches on the top of the beams. Use a mallet to knock the components into place, and to knock the top of the posts hard up against the outside faces of the end joists.

8 Set the ready-made trellis panels (F) in position between neighbouring frames and screw them to the posts.

Note: although we designed the size of the pergola around trellis panels 610 mm (24¹⁄₆₄ in) in width, you could easily modify the design to suit panels of a different width.

9 One piece at a time, slide a bracket (E) into place, hard up against the underside of a beam and through a spacer post. Check for squareness and screw it in place.

Note: you can fix the whole structure in place in the garden with metal foot sockets or with metal spikes running down into the ground. Give the whole structure a swift rub-down with the sander – just enough to remove splinters. Finally, give the whole structure a coat of exterior paint.

SUN LOUNGER

Now at last you can enjoy relaxing in the garden … no more perching on one of those cheap, nasty, plastic seats, or trying to make sense of an uncomfortable stick-and-canvas, rat-trap type of chair. This project draws inspiration from the beautiful teak and brass 'steamer' loungers that they had on ocean-going liners in the first quarter of the 19th century. Just imagine – the sun is shining, and there you are in the garden nicely stretched out on the lounger; the backrest is perfectly adjusted for maximum comfort, and your drink and book are comfortably to hand on the sliding table.

YOU WILL NEED

- Compasses
- Jigsaw
- Compound mitre saw
- Router and 6 mm (¼ in) round-over cutter
- Drill and twist bits to suit your screws, bolts and threaded rod
- Cordless driver, screwdriver bit to fit your screws, counter-bore bit and a countersink bit
- Orbital sander and 80-grit sandpaper
- 2 G-clamps
- Crosshead screwdriver
- Pine:
  A 2 pieces, 1949 x 90 x 40 mm (76¾ x 3¹⁷/₃₂ x 1⁹/₁₆ in)
  B 2 pieces, 318 x 90 x 40 mm (12¹⁷/₃₂ x 3¹⁷/₃₂ x 1⁹/₁₆ in)
  C 2 pieces, 350 x 90 x 40 mm (13²⁵/₃₂ x 3¹⁷/₃₂ x 1⁹/₁₆ in)
  D 18 pieces, 610 x 70 x 18 mm (24¹/₆₄ x 2¾ x ²³/₃₂ in)
  E 1 piece, 610 x 144 x 18 mm (24¹/₆₄ x 5²¹/₃₂ x ²³/₃₂ in)
  F 2 pieces, 645 x 64 x 40 mm (13¹³/₃₂ x 2¹⁷/₃₂ x 1⁹/₁₆ in)
  G 4 pieces, 610 x 70 x 18 mm (24¹/₆₄ x 2¾ x ²³/₃₂ in)
  H 2 pieces, 530 x 70 x 18 mm (20⅞ x 2¾ x ²³/₃₂ in)
  I 2 pieces, 215 x 35 x 18 mm (8¹⁵/₃₂ x 1⅜ x ²³/₃₂ in)
  J 1 piece, 450 x 70 x 18 mm (17²³/₃₂ x 2¾ x ²³/₃₂ in)
  K 2 pieces, 420 x 70 x 18 mm (16¹⁷/₃₂ x 2¾ x ²³/₃₂ in)
  L 4 pieces, 610 x 35 x 18 mm (24¹/₆₄ x 1⅜ x ²³/₃₂ in)
  M 10 pieces, 409 x 35 x 18 mm (16³/₃₂ x 1⅜ x ²³/₃₂ in)
- 2 x coach bolts, 100 mm (3¹⁵/₁₆ in) long, each with a wing nut and washer to fit
- 2 wheels, 120 mm (4²³/₃₂ in) in diameter
- Threaded rod: approx. 610 mm (24¹/₆₄ in) long and 10 mm (¹³/₃₂ in) in diameter, with 4 nuts and 4 washers to fit
- Crossheaded screws, No. 8:
  50 x 30 mm (1³¹/₃₂ x 1³/₁₆ in) long, 90 x 40 mm (3¹⁷/₃₂ x 1⁹/₁₆ in) long and 16 x 70 mm (⅝ x 2¾ in) long
- Wood-coloured filler
- Wood stain/preservative of your choice
- Wax polish
- Paintbrush

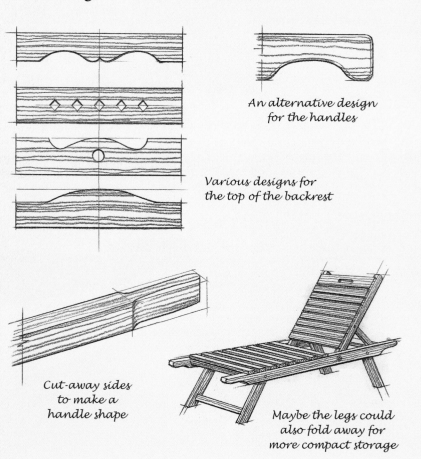

design variations

An alternative design for the handles

Various designs for the top of the backrest

Cut-away sides to make a handle shape

Maybe the legs could also fold away for more compact storage

Construction time: 3 weekends

Power tools required: compound mitre saw, jigsaw, router, drill, cordless driver and orbital sander

SUN LOUNGER CONSTRUCTION DRAWING

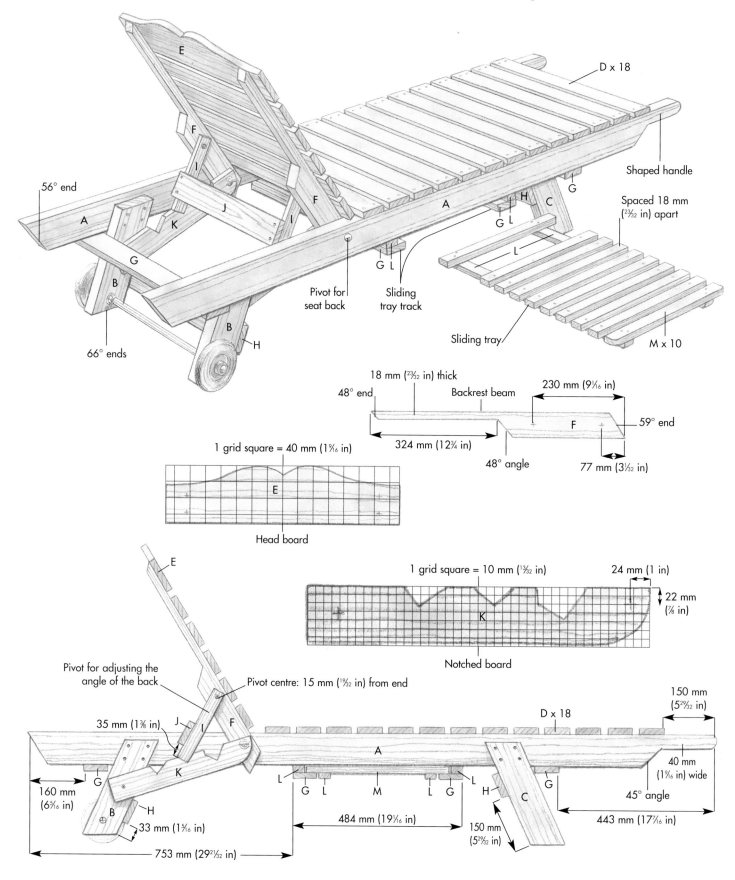

D x 18

Shaped handle

56° end

A

B

66° ends

B

G

H

F

I

J

K

G

F

I

Pivot for
seat back

G   L

G   L

H

A

G

C

Sliding
tray track

Sliding tray

Spaced 18 mm
($^{23}\!/_{32}$ in) apart

L

M x 10

18 mm ($^{23}\!/_{32}$ in) thick

48° end

Backrest beam

230 mm (9$^{1}\!/_{16}$ in)

324 mm (12$^{3}\!/_{4}$ in)

48° angle

F

77 mm (3$^{1}\!/_{32}$ in)

59° end

1 grid square = 40 mm (1$^{9}\!/_{16}$ in)

E

Head board

1 grid square = 10 mm (1$^{13}\!/_{32}$ in)

24 mm (1 in)

22 mm
($^{7}\!/_{8}$ in)

K

Notched board

E

Pivot for adjusting the
angle of the back

Pivot centre: 15 mm ($^{19}\!/_{32}$ in) from end

35 mm (1$^{3}\!/_{8}$ in)

J   I   F

K

160 mm
(6$^{5}\!/_{16}$ in)

B

G

H

33 mm (1$^{5}\!/_{16}$ in)

753 mm (29$^{21}\!/_{32}$ in)

G   L

L   M   L

G   L

H

C

G

484 mm (19$^{1}\!/_{16}$ in)

150 mm
(5$^{29}\!/_{32}$ in)

A

D x 18

150 mm
(5$^{29}\!/_{32}$ in)

40 mm
(1$^{9}\!/_{16}$ in) wide

45° angle

443 mm (17$^{7}\!/_{16}$ in)

HOW TO BUILD THE SUN LOUNGER

1 Use the compound mitre saw to cut all the pieces to length – the two long stretcher beams (A), the four legs (B, C), the 18 slats (D), and all the other components. Take the two stretcher beams a piece at a time, and draw the shape of the handle. Use the jigsaw to fret out the profile.

2 Secure the beams (A) side by side in the vice, fit the 6 mm (¼ in) round-over cutter in the router, and run a curve right around both components – from top to bottom and on both sides. Pay particular attention to the handles. Repeat this procedure with the legs (I) and side beams (F) that make the adjustable backrest.

3 Take the four legs – the wheel-end pair (B) are slightly shorter than those on the handle end (C) – and check that they are cut to the right angle on the mitre saw and nicely rounded with the router. Drill the holes for the fixing screws. Countersink the holes so that the screws fit flush.

4 Set the two stretcher beams (A) side by side and link them with the slats (D) using 40 mm (1⁹⁄₁₆ in) screws. Observe how the thickness of a slat can be used to regulate the spacing. **Note:** our way of working involves trial fittings. We might dry-fit and remove various parts several times before we are happy that they are right.

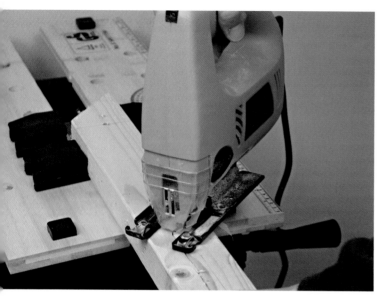

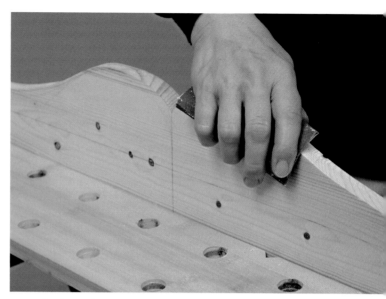

5 Use the mitre saw to cut the two backrest beams (F) to size, then establish the precise position of the pivot points for the bolts. Drill the pivot holes. Have a last check against the drawing to make sure that all is correct, and use the jigsaw to cut away the waste.

6 Take the wide board that goes to make the headboard (E), and use the jigsaw to fret out the traditional cyma curve 'lips' profile. Use the orbital sander to remove the corners, then use a piece of hand-held sandpaper to rub down the curves to a smooth, good-to-hold finish.

7 Assemble the seat back; use 30 mm (1¾₆ in) and 40 mm (1⅜₆ in) screws to attach the slats (D) and the headboard (E) to the backrest beams (F) (the 30 mm (1¾₆ in) screws are for the thin part of the backrest beams). Use the bolts, washers and wing nuts to pivot the two backrest beams (F) in position on the two stretcher beams (A). Turn the lounger over and attach the stretchers and sliding tray rack (G, L) using 40 mm (1⅜₆ in) screws. Mark out the shape of the notched board (K) using the grid as a guide. Attach the notched board and pivoting support (I, J). Make the tray (L, M) using 30 mm (1¾₆ in) screws.

8 Attach the legs (B, C) and the strengthening stretchers (H). Note how the top end of the leg is located just short of the cut-away angle at the back of the backrest beam, while the back edge of the leg is supported by the stretcher (G). Fill the screw holes (optional), allow to dry and use the orbital sander to clean and smooth all the surfaces.

9 Paint the whole lounger with stain/preservative (or paint), wait for it to dry, then ease and adjust the tray until it is a smooth-sliding fit. This procedure might involve loosening screws or removing built-up areas of paint.

10 Ease and adjust the backrest mechanism by loosening screws and bolts or removing built-up areas of paint. Apply some wax polish to the side of the backrest beams (F) to make adjustment easier.

TIPS AND TROUBLESHOOTING

Sliding tray If you like the overall design but want to cut down on the workload, you could miss out the sliding tray.

Handles and wheels If you want to cut costs, you could have handles at both ends – like a stretcher – then you wouldn't need to go to the trouble and expense of fitting the wheels.

Hardwood You could go for a more up-market design by using a home-grown hardwood like oak or ash. Don't be tempted to use a precious endangered wood like mahogany.

Child safety If you are worried about your children getting their fingers caught in the hinged mechanism, you could build in some sort of safety lock.

DOG KENNEL

This dog kennel draws its inspiration from a kennel that my grandparents had in their large country garden. Strangely enough, while I know for sure that they had chickens, geese, birds, bats, cats, mice and rats, I cannot remember them ever having a dog. Anyway, the lack of a dog did not hold me back, because I was either trying to entice dogs home in the vain hope that they would take up residence, or busy playing with an imaginary dog. The good news is that I now have a kennel complete with two real live dogs. The design is so straightforward that, while this kennel is designed for a small dog, you can easily modify the size to suit.

YOU WILL NEED

- Compasses
- Jigsaw
- Compound mitre saw
- Drill and counter-bore bit
- Cordless driver and screwdriver bit to fit your screws
- Orbital sander and 80-grit sandpaper
- 2 G-clamps
- Claw hammer
- Staple gun
- Coping saw
- Tenon saw
- Craft knife
- Pine:
  A 14 pieces, 460 x 32 x 32 mm (18⅛ x 1¼ x 1¼ in)
  B 2 pieces, 202 x 32 x 32 mm (7¹⁵⁄₁₆ x 1¼ x 1¼ in)
  C 4 pieces, 162 x 32 x 32 mm (6⅜ x 1¼ x 1¼ in)
  D 4 pieces, 150 x 32 x 32 mm (5²⁹⁄₃₂ x 1¼ x 1¼ in)
  E 4 pieces, 610 x 32 x 32 mm (24¹⁄₆₄ x 1¼ x 1¼ in)
  F 4 pieces, 400 x 32 x 32 mm (15¾ x 1¼ x 1¼ in)
  G 6 pieces, 921 x 32 x 32 mm (36¼ x 1¼ x 1¼ in)
  H 2 pieces, 985 x 70 x 18 mm (38²⁵⁄₃₂ x 2¾ x ²³⁄₃₂ in)
  I 4 pieces, 453 x 145 x 18 mm (17²⁷⁄₃₂ x 5²³⁄₃₂ x ²³⁄₃₂ in)
  J 1 piece, 453 x 86 x 18 mm (17²⁷⁄₃₂ x 3⅜ x ²³⁄₃₂ in)
  K 2 pieces, 985 x 25 x 8 mm (38²⁵⁄₃₂ x ³¹⁄₃₂ x ⁵⁄₁₆ in)

- Pine tongue-and-groove boards:
  L 12 pieces, 678 x 88 x 8 mm (26¹¹⁄₁₆ x 3¹⁵⁄₃₂ x ⁵⁄₁₆ in)
  M 16 pieces, 524 x 88 x 8 mm (20⅝ x 3¹⁵⁄₃₂ x ⁵⁄₁₆ in)
  N 12 pieces, 985 x 88 x 8 mm (38²⁵⁄₃₂ x 3¹⁵⁄₃₂ x ⁵⁄₁₆ in)

- 30 mm (1³⁄₁₆ in) pins
- Crossheaded screws: 64 x No. 8, 40 mm (1⁹⁄₁₆ in) long
- Organic paint of your choice
- Paintbrush
- Plastic sheet: 6 pieces, approximately 1000 x 1000 mm (39⅜ x 39⅜ in)

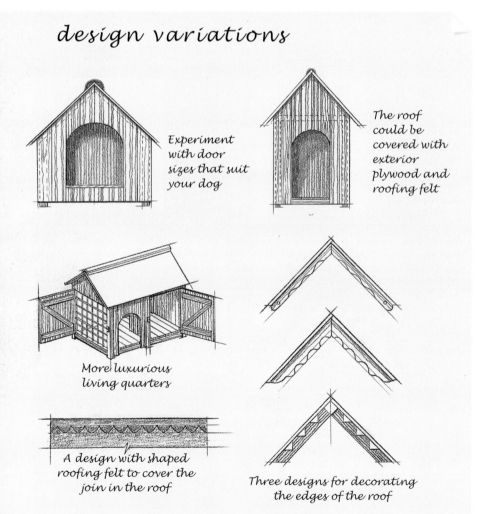

design variations

Experiment with door sizes that suit your dog

The roof could be covered with exterior plywood and roofing felt

More luxurious living quarters

A design with shaped roofing felt to cover the join in the roof

Three designs for decorating the edges of the roof

Construction time: 2 weekends

Power tools required: compound mitre saw, cordless driver, drill, jigsaw and orbital sander

4 Take a look at the construction drawings and see how the roof boards (N) are lapped one over another like the tiles on a roof. Have a real close-up look at this photograph, and note how the first board (on the far right) is raised up with a thin strip of wood (K). Construct the roof panels from F, G, N and K.

5 Use a pencil, ruler and compass to mark in the position of the door on the front panel, with the sides of the door lined up with the sides of the frame. Cut out the shape with the jigsaw and use sandpaper to rub down the cut edges to a smooth finish.

6 Run screw holes through the verticals (A) on the long panels, and screw the four wall panels together to make the basic box form. Make sure that the screws are clenched up tightly, so that the cladding all but meets at the corners.

7 Being mindful that the floorboards need to be a loose, easy fit so that they can be removed for cleaning, cut the boards to size and have a trial fitting. When you are happy with the fit, use the sander to rub all the surfaces to a smooth finish. Set the boards in place within the box form.

8 Draw the precise shape and position of the beam location notches – four on each of the two end panels. Cut out the notches with the coping saw. Set the two roof panels in position so that there is a generous overhang at the door end, and screw them in place. Staple a strip of plastic over the ridge so that the length of ridge joint is covered, and pin the two ridge boards (H) in place. Fix the boards at the end and to each other along their length. Rub down the whole kennel to remove sharp edges and splinters, and give all surfaces, inside and out, a couple of coats of animal-friendly paint. We have chosen an organic paint, but you could use any child-friendly paint.

4 Fit the drill with the flat bit. Mark in the position of the dowels on the top face of the seat slab (A) and the underside of the arms (E). Clamp the workpiece to the bench, and drill blind holes halfway through the thickness of the wood.

5 Have a dry-run fitting and mark in the position of all the screw holes. When you have checked and double-checked the position of the screw holes, fit the cordless driver with the counter-bore bit and run them through so that there is a pilot hole and a recess for the screw head and plug.

6 Use the orbital sander and the 80-grit sandpaper to clean off pencil marks and to smooth the surfaces of all the components. Assemble the sides, front and back, and check that the chair frame sits squarely on level ground. Make adjustments (relocate screws) if necessary.

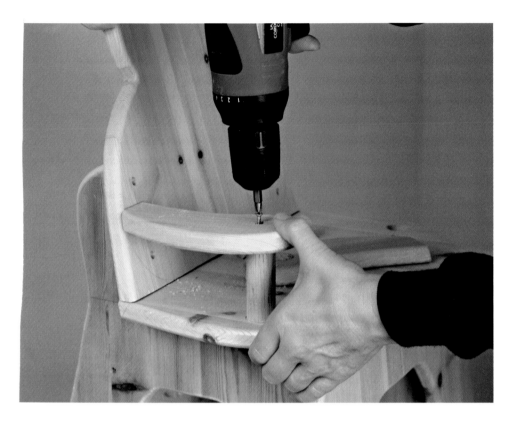

7 Screw the seat slab and back to the frame. Glue the dowels (F) into the holes in the seat. Glue and screw the end of the arms (E) to the back slab. Position the dowels so that they are well placed and captured between the seat and arms. Check the alignment and fix with screws. Plug the screw holes and rub down all surfaces to a smooth finish using the 600-grit sandpaper.

8 Apply one coat of high-gloss yacht varnish to the whole chair, allow to dry, then lightly sand to remove any roughness. Draw the face shapes on tracing paper and transfer the design to the wood (turn the tracing paper over and trace over the design to transfer the pencil lines). Paint each area, allow to dry and apply a final coat of varnish.

TIPS AND TROUBLESHOOTING

Plywood If you want to go for a stronger and lighter option, you could use top-grade plywood.

Router If you don't have a router you could give the routing procedures a miss and use sandpaper to rub down the edges of the cut-outs to a smooth finish.

Wood plugs If you don't like the notion of using wood plugs, you could use countersunk brass screws. If you go for this option, make sure that the screw heads are smooth to the touch – no sharp edges or whiskers of metal.

Paint It's vital to use safe, child-friendly paint. Check with your supplier.

REFERENCE CHARTS

COMMON SIZES FOR PLYWOOD

Length	Width	Thickness
2440 mm	1220 mm	6 mm
96 in	48 in	$\frac{1}{4}$ in
2440 mm	1220 mm	9 mm
96 in	48 in	$\frac{11}{32}$ in
2440 mm	1220 mm	12 mm
96 in	48 in	$\frac{15}{32}$ in
2440 mm	1220 mm	18 mm
96 in	48 in	$\frac{23}{32}$ in
1220 mm	607 mm	6 mm
48 in	$23\frac{29}{32}$ in	$\frac{1}{4}$ in
1220 mm	607 mm	9 mm
48 in	$23\frac{29}{32}$ in	$\frac{11}{32}$ in
1220 mm	607 mm	12 mm
48 in	$23\frac{29}{32}$ in	$\frac{15}{32}$ in
1220 mm	607 mm	18 mm
48 in	$23\frac{29}{32}$ in	$\frac{23}{32}$ in
1827 mm	607 mm	6 mm
$71\frac{15}{16}$ in	$23\frac{29}{32}$ in	$\frac{1}{4}$ in
1827 mm	607 mm	9 mm
$71\frac{15}{16}$ in	$23\frac{29}{32}$ in	$\frac{11}{32}$ in
1827 mm	607 mm	12 mm
$71\frac{15}{16}$ in	$23\frac{29}{32}$ in	$\frac{15}{32}$ in
2440 mm	607 mm	12 mm
96 in	$23\frac{29}{32}$ in	$\frac{15}{32}$ in
2440 mm	607 mm	18 mm
96 in	$23\frac{29}{32}$ in	$\frac{23}{32}$ in

COMMON SIZES FOR ROUGH-SAWN SOFTWOOD

Width	Thickness	Length
32 mm	19 mm	1800 mm
$1\frac{1}{4}$ in	$\frac{3}{4}$ in	$70\frac{7}{8}$ in
32 mm	19 mm	2400 mm
$1\frac{1}{4}$ in	$\frac{3}{4}$ in	$94\frac{1}{2}$ in
47 mm	22 mm	1800 mm
$1\frac{27}{32}$ in	$\frac{7}{8}$ in	$70\frac{7}{8}$ in
47 mm	22 mm	2400 mm
$1\frac{27}{32}$ in	$\frac{7}{8}$ in	$94\frac{1}{2}$ in
47 mm	47 mm	2400 mm
$1\frac{27}{32}$ in	$1\frac{27}{32}$ in	$94\frac{1}{2}$ in
47 mm	47 mm	3000 mm
$1\frac{27}{32}$ in	$1\frac{27}{32}$ in	$118\frac{1}{8}$ in
75 mm	47 mm	2400 mm
$2\frac{15}{16}$ in	$1\frac{27}{32}$ in	$94\frac{1}{2}$ in
75 mm	47 mm	3000 mm
$2\frac{15}{16}$ in	$1\frac{27}{32}$ in	$118\frac{1}{8}$ in
75 mm	47 mm	3600 mm
$2\frac{15}{16}$ in	$1\frac{27}{32}$ in	$141\frac{23}{32}$ in
100 mm	47 mm	2400 mm
$3\frac{15}{16}$ in	$1\frac{27}{32}$ in	$94\frac{1}{2}$ in
100 mm	47 mm	3000 mm
$3\frac{15}{16}$ in	$1\frac{27}{32}$ in	$118\frac{1}{8}$ in
100 mm	47 mm	3600 mm
$3\frac{15}{16}$ in	$1\frac{27}{32}$ in	$141\frac{23}{32}$ in
150 mm	47 mm	3600 mm
$5\frac{29}{32}$ in	$1\frac{27}{32}$ in	$141\frac{23}{32}$ in

COMMON SIZES FOR PLANED SOFTWOOD

Width	Thickness	Length
32 mm	12 mm	2100 mm
$1\frac{1}{4}$ in	$\frac{15}{32}$ in	$82\frac{11}{16}$ in
44 mm	12 mm	2400 mm
$1\frac{23}{32}$ in	$\frac{15}{32}$ in	$94\frac{1}{2}$ in
28 mm	18 mm	1800 mm
$1\frac{3}{32}$ in	$\frac{23}{32}$ in	$70\frac{7}{8}$ in
28 mm	18 mm	2400 mm
$1\frac{3}{32}$ in	$\frac{23}{32}$ in	$94\frac{1}{2}$ in
44 mm	18 mm	1800 mm
$1\frac{23}{32}$ in	$\frac{23}{32}$ in	$70\frac{7}{8}$ in
44 mm	18 mm	2400 mm
$1\frac{23}{32}$ in	$\frac{23}{32}$ in	$94\frac{1}{2}$ in
69 mm	18 mm	2400 mm
$2\frac{23}{32}$ in	$\frac{23}{32}$ in	$94\frac{1}{2}$ in
94 mm	18 mm	2400 mm
$3\frac{11}{16}$ in	$\frac{23}{32}$ in	$94\frac{1}{2}$ in
119 mm	18 mm	2400 mm
$4\frac{11}{16}$ in	$\frac{23}{32}$ in	$94\frac{1}{2}$ in
144 mm	18 mm	1800 mm
$5\frac{21}{32}$ in	$\frac{23}{32}$ in	$70\frac{7}{8}$ in
144 mm	18 mm	2400 mm
$5\frac{21}{32}$ in	$\frac{23}{32}$ in	$94\frac{1}{2}$ in
44 mm	20 mm	2400 mm
$1\frac{23}{32}$ in	$\frac{25}{32}$ in	$94\frac{1}{2}$ in
34 mm	34 mm	1800 mm
$1\frac{11}{32}$ in	$1\frac{11}{32}$ in	$70\frac{7}{8}$ in
34 mm	34 mm	2400 mm
$1\frac{11}{32}$ in	$1\frac{11}{32}$ in	$94\frac{1}{2}$ in
44 mm	34 mm	1800 mm
$1\frac{23}{32}$ in	$1\frac{11}{32}$ in	$70\frac{7}{8}$ in
44 mm	34 mm	2400 mm
$1\frac{23}{32}$ in	$1\frac{11}{32}$ in	$94\frac{1}{2}$ in
69 mm	34 mm	2400 mm
$2\frac{23}{32}$ in	$1\frac{11}{32}$ in	$94\frac{1}{2}$ in
44 mm	44 mm	1800 mm
$1\frac{23}{32}$ in	$1\frac{23}{32}$ in	$70\frac{7}{8}$ in
69 mm	44 mm	1800 mm
$2\frac{23}{32}$ in	$1\frac{23}{32}$ in	$70\frac{7}{8}$ in
94 mm	44 mm	2400 mm
$3\frac{11}{16}$ in	$1\frac{23}{32}$ in	$94\frac{1}{2}$ in
69 mm	69 mm	2400 mm
$2\frac{23}{32}$ in	$2\frac{23}{32}$ in	$94\frac{1}{2}$ in

Construction time: 2 weekends

Power tools required: jigsaw, router, drill, cordless driver and orbital sander

CHILD'S TEDDY BEAR CHAIR CONSTRUCTION DRAWING

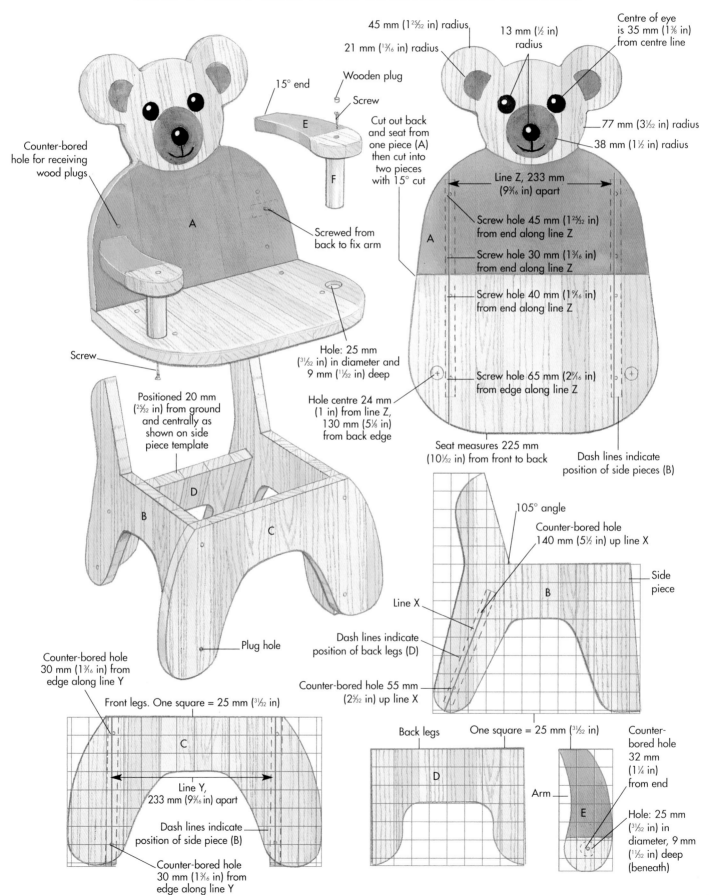

45 mm (1²⁵⁄₃₂ in) radius

21 mm (¹³⁄₁₆ in) radius

13 mm (½ in) radius

Centre of eye is 35 mm (1⅜ in) from centre line

15° end

Wooden plug

Screw

Counter-bored hole for receiving wood plugs

77 mm (3³⁄₃₂ in) radius

38 mm (1½ in) radius

Cut out back and seat from one piece (A) then cut into two pieces with 15° cut

Line Z, 233 mm (9³⁄₁₆ in) apart

Screw hole 45 mm (1²⁵⁄₃₂ in) from end along line Z

Screw hole 30 mm (1³⁄₁₆ in) from end along line Z

Screwed from back to fix arm

Screw hole 40 mm (1⁹⁄₁₆ in) from end along line Z

Screw

Hole: 25 mm (³¹⁄₃₂ in) in diameter and 9 mm (¹¹⁄₃₂ in) deep

Screw hole 65 mm (2⁹⁄₁₆ in) from edge along line Z

Positioned 20 mm (²⁵⁄₃₂ in) from ground and centrally as shown on side piece template

Hole centre 24 mm (1 in) from line Z, 130 mm (5⅛ in) from back edge

Seat measures 225 mm (10¹⁄₃₂ in) from front to back

Dash lines indicate position of side pieces (B)

105° angle

Counter-bored hole 140 mm (5½ in) up line X

Line X

Side piece

Dash lines indicate position of back legs (D)

Plug hole

Counter-bored hole 55 mm (2³⁄₃₂ in) up line X

Counter-bored hole 30 mm (1³⁄₁₆ in) from edge along line Y

Front legs. One square = 25 mm (³¹⁄₃₂ in)

Back legs

One square = 25 mm (³¹⁄₃₂ in)

Counter-bored hole 32 mm (1¼ in) from end

Line Y, 233 mm (9³⁄₁₆ in) apart

Arm

Dash lines indicate position of side piece (B)

Counter-bored hole 30 mm (1³⁄₁₆ in) from edge along line Y

Hole: 25 mm (³¹⁄₃₂ in) in diameter, 9 mm (¹¹⁄₃₂ in) deep (beneath)

INDEX